AIR CAMPAIGN

RABAUL 1943–44

Reducing Japan's great island fortress

MARK LARDAS | ILLUSTRATED BY MARK POSTLETHWAITE

Osprey Publishing
c/o Bloomsbury Publishing Plc
PO Box 883, Oxford, OX1 9PL, UK
Or
c/o Bloomsbury Publishing Inc.
1385 Broadway, 5th Floor, New York, NY 10018, USA
E-mail: info@ospreypublishing.com

www.ospreypublishing.com

OSPREY is a trademark of Osprey Publishing Ltd, a division of Bloomsbury Publishing Plc.

First published in Great Britain in 2018

A CIP catalogue record for this book is available from the British Library.

ISBN: PB: 9781472822444
           ePub: 9781472822451
           ePDF: 9781472822437
           XML 9781472822468

18 19 20 21 22   10 9 8 7 6 5 4 3 2 1

Index by Zoe Ross
Typeset in Adobe Garamond Pro, Futura Std, Sabon and Akzidenz-Grotesk Condensed
3D diagrams by Adam Tooby
Cartography by bounford.com
3D BEVs by The Black Spot
Printed in China through World Print Ltd.

Artist's note

Readers may care to note that the original paintings from which the colour plates in this book were prepared are available for private sale. All reproduction copyright whatsoever is retained by the Publishers. All enquiries should be addressed to: mark@posart.com
The Publishers regret that they can enter into no correspondence upon this matter.

Front Cover: Art © Osprey Publishing
Back Cover: Photo courtesy USNHHC

Osprey Publishing supports the Woodland Trust, the UK's leading woodland conservation charity. Between 2014 and 2018 our donations are being spent on their Centenary Woods project in the UK.

To find out more about our authors and books visit www.ospreypublishing.com. Here you will find extracts, author interviews, details of forthcoming events and the option to sign up for our newsletter.

Author's Note
The following abbreviations indicate the sources of the illustrations used in this volume:
AC – Author's Collection
LOC – Library of Congress, Washington, DC
USNHHC – United States Navy Heritage and History Command

Author's Dedication
I would like to dedicate this book to my good friend, Jim Oberg, and to his uncle, Lieutenant Albert Oberg, who gave his last full measure of devotion aboard the USS *Strong* in July 1943 in the Solomon Islands during the run up to the events described in this book.

CONTENTS

INTRODUCTION

Simpson Harbor gave Rabaul one of the finest anchorages in the Pacific. Large, deep, and sheltered, it could anchor a fleet, and the largest ship could anchor close to shore. This picture shows Simpson Harbor in early 1943. (USAAF)

Simpson Harbor has the finest anchorage in the Southwest Pacific. Set on the eastern end of New Britain, it is a marvelous deep-water harbor, 2 miles wide by 4 miles long, with water depths of 8 fathoms literally a stone's throw from the shore. The depth through much of the harbor exceeds 27 fathoms. Simpson Harbor is protected on three sides by volcanic mountains, with the entrance to the harbor emptying into Blanche Bay. Blanche Bay's entrance to the ocean lies some 45 degrees from the main axis of Simpson Harbor. This entrance feeds into a channel roughly perpendicular to Blanche Bay, formed by the sheltering ridges of New Britain and New Ireland. The result is an anchorage deep enough for the greatest draft ship ever built, and large enough to accommodate the world's largest fleet within a sheltered haven.

Since its creation by a violent volcanic explosion in the seventh century AD, Simpson Harbor was largely overlooked by everyone except those native to New Britain or neighboring islands, such as New Ireland. It came to the attention of the outside world in 1872 when the frigate HMS *Blanche*, commanded by Captain Cortland Simpson, surveyed the waters around New Britain. Simpson named the harbor for himself and the larger bay for his ship. Twelve years later, in 1884, New Britain, New Ireland, the northern Solomon Islands, and the northeastern quarter of New Guinea were annexed by Germany, becoming German New Guinea. Taking advantage of the magnificent harbor, the Germans built the province's capital on the north end of Simpson Harbor, naming the town Rabaul.

German rule ended in 1914. After World War I started Australian troops captured Rabaul. Following the war's end the League of Nations mandated control of German New Guinea to Australia. Australia renamed all of the islands, retaining only the German name for the sea north of New Britain. It remained the Bismarck Sea.

Rabaul was still the capital of the Mandate territory, but experienced relatively little growth. The town was in an active volcano zone and minor eruptions were frequent. In 1937, Tavurvur and Vulcan, two volcanoes near Rabaul, exploded, killing over 500 and flattening the town. The territorial capital was moved to Lae, on New Guinea. Volcanoes made the town too dangerous for a territorial governor, but the harbor was simply too good to abandon. Rabaul remained the most important town in New Britain.

Simpson Harbor, despite its excellence, was in the wrong place for Australia to use it much. The port was not on the way to anywhere, on an isolated island far from trade routes. Rabaul would never become a Singapore or a Hong Kong. Between 1918 and 1941 Rabaul remained a backwater; a place for copra planters on New Britain to ship their product to market. Australia committed relatively little to the development or defense of Rabaul. The Australians built an airstrip at Lakunai, on the southeast corner of Rabaul, and a second, larger airstrip at Vunakanau, southwest of Vulcan volcano. Both were primitive airfields with grass runways and hardstands, and no revetments for their aircraft. Communications facilities were built, including a commercial radio station. A constabulary post was established.

On December 7, 1941, with the start of World War II in the Pacific, Rabaul's location gained significant strategic importance, especially for the Japanese, as they rampaged across the Pacific. The main Japanese base in the Central Pacific was at Truk, an atoll in the Caroline Islands. Rabaul was within 800 miles of Truk, well within the operational radius of American long-range bombers operating from Rabaul. True, the United States and its Australian allies had no long-range bombers at Rabaul in December 1941. Only ten obsolescent Wirraway fighters, four Hudson bombers, and the incongruously named 1,400-man Lark Force guarded Rabaul. But while Rabaul remained in Allied hands, Truk was threatened.

Rabaul was also within the operational radius of Japanese bombers based at Truk, and only two days' steaming for fast transports departing Truk. Japanese aircraft carriers from Truk could reach Rabaul still faster.

Japan soon moved against Rabaul. Truk-based bombers began bombing Rabaul shortly after New Year's Day. Two weeks later they were joined by carrier aircraft, starting a week-long campaign which routed the Royal Australian Air Force (RAAF) Wirraways and Hudsons. The Japanese landed on New Britain on January 22, and took Rabaul the next day. Lark Force had been ordered to hold off the Japanese for as long as possible and then run for safety. They slowed the Japanese not an hour and were swallowed whole within a week.

Rabaul was easily reached by long-range Japanese fighters, such as the Mitsubishi A6M "Zero," allowing any air garrison at a Japanese-held Rabaul to be quickly reinforced.

A Nakajima B5N (Allied code name "Kate") torpedo bomber takes off from the aircraft carrier *Shokaku* en route to Pearl Harbor on December 7, 1941. This torpedo-carrying aircraft played a major role in projecting Japanese power. (USNHHC)

Port Moresby was both a primary Japanese objective and the chief Allied base from which the offensive against Rabaul was launched. While less important by September 1944, it still played an important role in the October air offensive against Rabaul. (USAAF)

The port facilities were excellent, and the harbor big enough to hold the entire Imperial Japanese Navy, its fleet train, and enough transports and supply ships to carry and maintain an army corps.

Rabaul became the locus of Japanese expansion in the Southwest Pacific. It was perfectly placed to project power to the seas around northwest Australia. Lae and the Admiralty Islands were within 400 miles of Rabaul's airfields; Port Moresby only 500 miles away. Guadalcanal, at the southern end of the Solomons chain, was 650 statute miles by air from Rabaul.

Japan soon moved troops, aircraft, and resources to Rabaul. Not all stayed at Rabaul, passing to New Guinea or into the Solomons. But they staged through Rabaul, following a route from the Japanese homeland through the Marianas to Truk, and then Rabaul.

The battle of the Coral Sea, fought in May 1942, led the Japanese to call off a planned invasion of Port Moresby on the southern coast of New Guinea. Troops for the landing, at sea when the operation was canceled, had boarded transports in Simpson Harbor, and returned afterwards. By June 1942 Japan had 21,000 soldiers in Rabaul, and another 20,000 on the surrounding islands. Over 150 aircraft of all types operated from the two airfields captured from the Australians.

For the next six months the Japanese continued building up their forces at Rabaul. They expanded and improved the two airfields they had and began work on three others. They continued moving troops to and through Rabaul. Some went on to occupy the rest of New Britain. The Japanese set up airfields at six widely distributed spots on New Britain, with army garrisons to protect them. Some troops shifted to New Guinea. These forces were intended to push the Australians off the island, capturing Port Moresby by crossing the Owen Stanley Mountains. Many occupied islands around New Britain: the Solomons as far south as Guadalcanal, Kiriwina Island, and the Woodlark Islands.

Many more stayed, however. By the start of 1943 there were over 100,000 men scattered around the Gazelle Peninsula, where Rabaul was located. There were nearly 90,000 tons of supplies and 2.5 million gallons of gasoline and oil cached in Gazelle Peninsula dumps, most within 10 miles of Rabaul. Rabaul was the logistics center that fed the Japanese military in the Southwest Pacific.

The Japanese had also moved thousands of POWs and shiploads of "comfort girls" to Rabaul. The POWs served as laborers to build runways, roads, and buildings. The comfort girls, recruited under the pretense they were to become factory workers, were forced into prostitution serving the garrison.

The laborers were needed. While the runways on the rest of New Britain were grass strips, the Japanese paved runways on the two existing airports, and the three new ones. In 1942 and 1943 they added miles of paved roads throughout the Gazelle Peninsula. They threw up hangars, warehouses, barracks, radio shacks, control towers, repair facilities, docks, and the other facilities needed to maintain a modern army, navy, and air force. They also built lots of gun positions, both shore and antiaircraft batteries. Rabaul soon became more formidable than Truk, with more men, more guns, and more aircraft.

What it did not become was the springboard to Australia. The battle of the Coral Sea proved the high-water mark for the Japanese in the Southwest Pacific. They took Guadalcanal, but moved no further south. Nor did they make significant progress in New Guinea. Instead the Japanese were thrown on the defensive. In August 1942, US Marines landed on Guadalcanal, capturing the airfield the Japanese had just completed. A Japanese invasion at Milne Bay in late August 1942 was not only thrown back, but the attacking force was crushed.

The struggle on Guadalcanal continued until February 9, 1943, with the final six weeks a Japanese withdrawal. Japan lost 24,000 soldiers, 24 warships (including two battleships and an aircraft carrier), and nearly 700 aircraft at Guadalcanal. News from New Guinea was no better. After Milne Bay the Allies had gone on the offensive in New Guinea. Starting in November, Australian and US troops began a drive culminating in January 1943 with the capture of the Japanese base at Buna. By the start of 1943 Japan was on the defensive. Rabaul was the Allies' ultimate objective.

The extent to which the tide had shifted became apparent in the first half of 1943. Forces under the overall command of Admiral Bill Halsey began pushing up the Solomons chain, capturing the Russell Islands in February, and landing on New Georgia in July. By September, the pacification of New Georgia was complete, and the Japanese airfield at Munda controlled by the Allies. One of that campaign's casualties was the architect of the Pearl Harbor attack. Admiral Isoroku Yamamoto was killed when the bomber he was flying in was shot down over Buin, on April 18, 1943.

Admiral William "Bill" Halsey commanded the South Pacific Theater. Halsey directed Comairsols which did the heavy lifting in reducing Rabaul. He was the man who made the call to attack Rabaul with *Saratoga* and *Princeton*. (USNHHC)

OPPOSITE THE SOUTHWEST PACIFIC: STRATEGIC OVERVIEW

Things went as badly for the Japanese in New Guinea. Allied forces led by General Douglas MacArthur began pushing north from Buna. In January they repulsed a Japanese thrust against Wau in New Guinea's interior. The Allies began a long drive to recapture Lae, the territorial capital. The land acquired was used to build new airfields, allowing Allied aircraft to reach Rabaul without flying over the Owen Stanley Mountains.

The impact of these new airfields was felt in March, during the battle of the Bismarck Sea. The three-day battle saw B-25 Mitchells from the New Guinea-based Fifth Air Force destroy a Japanese convoy carrying reinforcements to New Guinea. All eight transports were sunk, as were four of the eight escorting destroyers. In June MacArthur's forces took the Woodlark Islands and Kiriwina, giving the Allies airfields close to New Britain. By September Lae and Finschhafen, formerly Japanese strongholds, were in Allied hands, their airfields turned against their previous owners.

As September drew to a close, Rabaul was the next target. Plans to retake Rabaul had been drawn up as early as July 1942. However by January 1943, land operations against the Japanese in New Guinea and the Solomon Islands demonstrated that Allied soldiers could expect stubborn resistance and heavy casualties against entrenched Japanese soldiers. No place in the Southwest Pacific had more, and more heavily entrenched, Japanese soldiers than did Rabaul and the Gazelle Peninsula. Invading them could prove prohibitively costly. Yet they could not be ignored.

Prior campaigns had used airpower to isolate and immobilize enemy forces, which were then mopped up by boots on the ground. Germany had done this in Norway and Crete. The Japanese had done it throughout the Pacific, but to greatest effect in the Philippines. The Allies had used this approach in the Solomons and New Guinea.

An alternative strategy had been developed in March. Instead of invading Rabaul, Rabaul would be neutralized by airpower. The Allies would seize lightly held islands around Rabaul, build airfields on them, and ring Rabaul with Allied aircraft. These aircraft, conducting sustained raids and patrols, would gradually reduce Rabaul to irrelevance as a military base.

This strategy had never been tried before by either side. If successful, this campaign would rewrite the rulebook. Up through September, the Allies had been preparing to lay siege to Rabaul by air. By October 1943, they were ready to see if airpower alone could neutralize a major enemy base.

Skip bombing, and the field modification of B-25s to give them strafing capabilities, transformed them into ship-killers. At the battle of the Bismarck Sea eight transports, including this one, and four destroyers were sunk by Fifth Air Force B-25s. (AC)

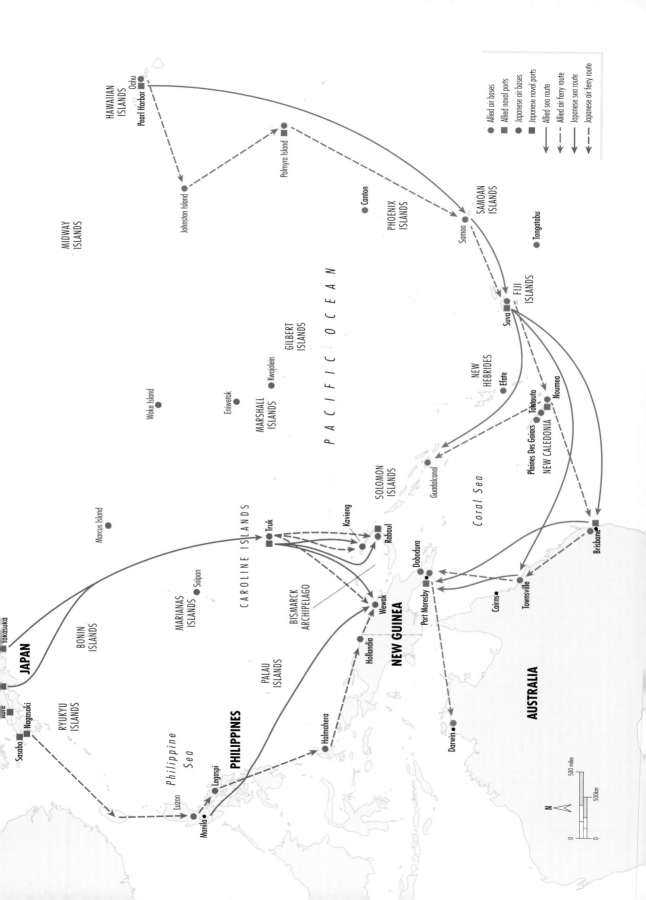

CHRONOLOGY

1942
January 23 Japanese capture Rabaul.

April 1 Japanese Eleventh Air Fleet units arrive at Rabaul.

July 2 The Joint Chiefs of Staff issue a directive calling for the recapture of Rabaul as Task Three of operations in the Southwest Pacific.

December 30 Rapopo airfield becomes operational.

1943
January 23 Casablanca Conference approves operations against Rabaul.

February 12 MacArthur develops *Elkton*, a plan to capture Rabaul.

February 15 Comairsols formed, unifying command of Allied air assets in the Solomon Islands.

February 28 MacArthur develops *Elkton II*, a revision of *Elkton*.

March 2–5 Battle of the Bismarck Sea: four Japanese destroyers and eight Japanese transports sunk by Fifth Air Force B-25s making low-level strikes.

March 28 Joint Chiefs of Staff cancels the July 2, 1942 directive, replacing it with a plan substituting isolation of Rabaul for invasion and occupation.

April 28 MacArthur approves *Elkton III* plan to bypass Rabaul.

June 23 Woodlark Islands captured by Allies.

June 30 Kiriwina captured by Allies.

August 5 Munda airfield on New Georgia captured by Allies.

August 14 Munda airfield becomes operational for Allies.

August 30 Tobera airfield on Rabaul becomes operational.

September 30 Construction of Keravat airfield begins, but the airfield never becomes fully operational.

October 12 Fifth Air Force begins air offensive to neutralize Rabaul. The initial raid involves 339 aircraft attacking Vunakanau, Rapopo, and Tobera airfields.

October 15 Fifteen Vals accompanied by 39 Zeroes from Rabaul launch airstrike against shipping in Oro Bay, New Guinea intending to interdict supplies going to Dobodura airfield. Fourteen Vals and five Zeroes are shot down.

October 17 Fifty-six Zeroes conduct a fighter sweep against Dobodura airfield. Eight Zeroes, four P-38s, and one P-40 are shot down. It is the last Rabaul-based attack against New Guinea airfields.

October 18 Fifth Air Force launches 77 B-24s, 54 B-25s, and 90 P-38s on an airstrike against Rabaul airfields. Bad weather causes all but the B-25s to return without attacking.

October 20 Aircraft from the 1st Carrier Division ordered from Truk to Rabaul to participate in Operation *RO*, reinforcing Rabaul with another 300 aircraft.

October 23–25 The Fifth Air Force launches daily attacks against the four operational Rabaul airfields. Each attack involves at least 100 aircraft.

ABOVE On October 18, 1943 while off Vunapope the Japanese subchaser CH-23 was attacked by a B-25 from the 345rd Bomb Group. Two 1,000lb bombs blew its bow off. CH-23 was run aground and later repaired. (USAAF)

October 29 59 B-24s escorted by 81 P-38s from Fifth Air Force sortie for high-altitude attack on Vunakanau.

November 1 Allies invade Bougainville, taking the middle of the island to provide space for airfields.

November 1/2 Japanese attempt a counter-invasion at Bougainville, but transports are not ready. A Japanese task force of cruisers and destroyers sent to attack the US invasion fleet is defeated at the battle of Empress Augusta Bay by US Navy light cruisers and destroyers in a night action.

November 2 Japanese send 100 light bombers and fighters from Rabaul against the Bougainville invasion fleet. The attack causes minimal damage.

November 2 Seventy-two B-25 bombers and 80 P-38s fighters from the Fifth Air Force attack Simpson Harbor. The airstrike destroys or damages several warships and many of the invasion transports, and prevents follow-up Japanese airstrikes against Bougainville.

November 3 Seven heavy cruisers, one light cruiser, and four destroyers are sent from Truk to Rabaul to reinforce Japanese surface forces there.

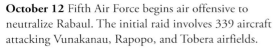

OPPOSITE The Japanese invested a lot of effort and material to upgrade Rabaul into a major operational base. Among the infrastructure improvements added were nearly 400 miles of new, paved road, such as that pictured here. (AC)

November 5 A carrier strike from *Saratoga* and *Princeton* hits Simpson Harbor shortly after Japanese reinforcements arrive at Rabaul. Seven cruisers are damaged, preventing the Japanese from attempting a night surface action against Bougainville.

November 5 Fifth Air Force launches an airstrike against Rabaul shortly after the Navy completes its airstrike. Based on estimates of Japanese aircraft destroyed, General Kenney declares Rabaul neutralized.

November 11 US Navy aircraft from *Essex*, *Bunker Hill*, *Independence*, *Saratoga*, and *Princeton* strike Rabaul, sinking or damaging four Japanese warships. Japanese counterstrikes are driven off with heavy loss to the Japanese, and little damage to the carrier strike group attacked.

November 12 Surviving aircraft of 1st Carrier Division are withdrawn, departing Rabaul for Truk.

November 14/15 Thirty-six Beauforts launch a nighttime torpedo attack against ships in Simpson Harbor.

December 10 Torokina airfield, Bougainville (fighter strip), becomes operational for Allied aircraft.

December 15 Arawe (on New Britain) is invaded, and the Japanese airfield there captured by US forces.

December 17 First Comairsols fighter sweep over Rabaul occurs, involving 80 Marine, Navy, and Royal New Zealand Air Force (RNZAF) aircraft.

December 23–30 Daily large-scale airstrikes are made against Rabaul by Comairsols bombers and fighters.

December 25 Aircraft from *Bunker Hill* and *Monterey* attack ships in Kavieng Harbor, facing minimal aerial opposition because its fighters were transferred to Rabaul due to an Allied feint.

BELOW The scene during the height of the November 5, 1943 carrier strike on Rabaul. Aircraft from *Saratoga* and *Princeton* hit Japanese cruisers in Simpson Harbor. Cruisers and destroyers exit Simpson Harbor with one heavy cruiser (right center) hit. (USNHHC)

December 26 Cape Gloucester invaded and Cape Gloucester airfield captured by US forces.

1944

January 2–9 Fighter sweeps and bombing by single-engine bombers is carried out against Rabaul, focusing on Japanese airfields.

January 9 Tobera airfield is temporarily closed by a bombing raid, the first time Allied bombing shuts down an airfield.

January 10 The bomber strip at Piva South airfield (Bougainville) becomes operational.

January 11 Comairsols B-25s attack Vunakanau airfield, the first B-25 attack launched from the Solomons.

January 14 Thirty-six SBDs and 16 TBDs attack Lakunai escorted by RNZAF P-40s and Marine F4Us. The attack is launched from Munda with refueling stop at Piva.

January 17 Comairsols begins launching almost daily heavy raids against Rabaul.

January 25 Sixth Attack Air Force is relieved by 2nd Carrier Division. Sixth Attack Air Force withdrawn to Truk.

February 10 Comairsols daily raids against Rabaul increase to over 200 aircraft per day.

February 15 Green Islands invaded and captured.

February 17–18 USN destroyers conduct night naval bombardment of Rabaul and Simpson Harbor.

February 18 Fifth Air Force raids knock out Kavieng airfields.

February 19 Rabaul installations attacked heavily by US Marine Corps (USMC), US Navy, and US Army Air Force (USAAF) aircraft.

February 21 Japanese abandon air defense of Rabaul, withdraw all remaining aircraft.

February 21 Convoy departing Rabaul is attacked and devastated by B-25s.

February 22 USN Destroyer Squadron 25 attacks and destroys remnants of convoy in surface action, marking naval isolation of New Britain.

February 25 Second naval bombardment of Rabaul.

February 29 Third naval bombardment of Rabaul.

February 29 Manus and Los Negros Islands in Admiralties invaded.

March 1 Comairsols begins bombing campaign to obliterate Rabaul city.

March 8 Nissan airfield (in Green Islands) operational.

March 9 Allied bombers begin unescorted missions to Rabaul.

March 20 Marines land on and occupy Emirau.

April 8 Daily raids against Japanese supply dumps cease due to a lack of targets.

April 14 Emirau airfield opens.

April 20 Daily mass raids against Rabaul city cease due to a lack of targets. City 90 percent destroyed.

April 21 on Small air raids continue over Gazelle Peninsula to keep Rabaul and its airfields suppressed. These continue through January 1945.

May 2 Emirau airfield operational.

1945

August 15 Japan unconditionally surrenders to Allied powers.

September 6 Japanese forces at Rabaul surrender to the Australians.

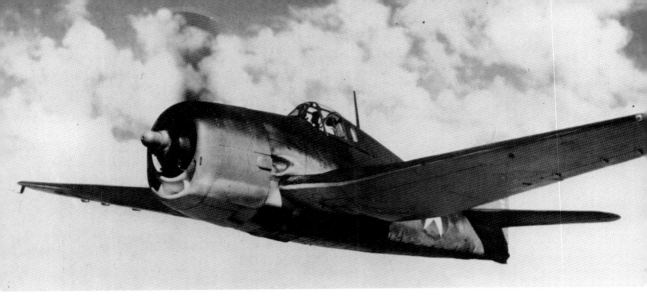

ATTACKERS' CAPABILITIES
Fifth Air Force and Comairsols

The Grumman F6F Hellcat was the fighter most feared by Japanese fighter pilots at Rabaul. It could not reach Rabaul until Allied airfields became available on Bougainville. (USNHHC)

Rabaul was at the junction of two major Allied Commands: the Southwest Pacific Area under Douglas MacArthur and the South Pacific Area commanded by William Halsey for Admiral Chester Nimitz. The South Pacific Area also contained significant US Army forces. The attack on Rabaul drew the resources of three independent air commands: the Fifth Air Force in MacArthur's command, the US Army Thirteenth Air Force (part of the South Pacific Command), and Navy and Marine Corps air assets in the Solomon Islands and surrounding territory. USAAF, Navy, and Marine aircraft in this region were consolidated into Comairsols (Command Air, Solomons), but cooperation between Comairsols and the Fifth Air Force had to be negotiated.

Allied success would depend upon Comairsols having sufficient aircraft with the right capabilities, an airbase infrastructure from which to launch a concentrated air assault on Rabaul, and the weapons and tactics to effectively destroy Japanese facilities, aircraft, and ships. Long-range bombers and fighters could reach Rabaul from existing airfields, but shorter-ranged, higher-performance single-engine fighters needed closer bases to operate over Rabaul, as did the specialist torpedo bombers and dive bombers. Between March and the start of October the Allies focused on developing infrastructure, both by constructing new and acquiring existing airfields and by reducing Japan's ability to attack these new airfields.

Aircraft were drawn from the Fifth and Thirteenth Air Forces of the USAAF. There were 13 land-based naval squadrons, 33 USMC squadrons, and 14 carrier-based naval squadrons on five aircraft carriers. During the first six months of 1943 US forces perfected new weapons and tactics, adding significantly to the air offensive against Rabaul which started in October 1943.

Aircraft in theater

Eight main aircraft types – five bomber and three fighter – were used by the Allied forces to reduce Rabaul. These were:

Consolidated B-24 Liberator

Called the PB4Y by the US Navy, the Liberator was a four-engine heavy bomber. It could carry up to 8,000lb of bombs internally, but its normal bomb load was 5,000lb. It had a maximum speed of 300mph, a cruising speed in formation of 180–210mph, and a range of 3,000 miles. Although it could be used as a medium- or low-level bomber, on bombing missions against Rabaul it was normally used as a high-level bomber, typically operating at 18,000–25,000ft. It was also used for reconnaissance or maritime patrol, particularly by the Navy and the Thirteenth Air Force. The Fifth Air Force deployed 12 B-24 squadrons; the Thirteenth Air Force seven, and the US Navy one squadron of PB4Ys, each squadron nominally with 12 aircraft. The Fifth Air Force could theoretically commit over 140 B-24s, but the most ever sent on a single raid was 90.

North American B-25 Mitchell

Called the PBJ when used by the US Navy or Marine Corps, the Mitchell was a twin-engine medium bomber. It carried up to 5,000lb of bombs and had a range of 3,000 miles, a top speed of 272mph and a cruising speed of 230mph. Most B-25s used in the campaign were field-modified to add eight forward-firing .50-caliber machine guns. The Mitchell was used primarily as a low-level attack bomber, particularly against airfields and shipping. After the Japanese defenses were suppressed it was used as a medium-level bomber against Rabaul city. The Fifth Air Force had eight 16-aircraft squadrons of B-25s, the Thirteenth Air Force six squadrons, the Navy four squadrons, and Marines five. The Fifth Air Force flew raids with as many as 75 B-25s in a single raid. Comairsols raids tended to use smaller numbers, typically 24–36. Despite its smaller size, the B-25 proved the decisive weapon in the campaign against Rabaul, as its combination of virtues was right for the low-level role. It was relatively maneuverable, carried a useful bomb load, and had the additional strafing punch of its eight .50-calibers.

B-25s with eight forward-firing .50-caliber machine guns were field modifications performed in New Guinea using machine guns from wrecked fighters. North American, the manufacturer, eventually built similar aircraft in their factory. The aircraft being serviced here on a Pacific island was factory-built. (AC)

Grumman TBF Avenger

The Avenger was a single-engine torpedo bomber used by the US Navy and the Marine Corps. It had a crew of three and could carry a single 18in aerial torpedo or 2,000lb of bombs. It had a range of 1,000 miles, a top speed of 275mph, a cruising speed of 145mph, and a service ceiling of 30,000ft. The Avenger was operated by both land-based and carrier-based squadrons. Used as a torpedo bomber during the early phases of the Rabaul campaign, it was later used as a medium-altitude or high-altitude level bomber, when few ships worth a torpedo remained near New Britain. Three shore-based naval squadrons, five shore-based Marine squadrons, and five carrier-based Avenger squadrons were used during the campaign.

Douglas SBD Dauntless and Curtiss SB2C Helldiver

These were two single-engine dive bombers used by Navy and Marine squadrons during the campaign. The Dauntless could carry up to 2,250lb of bombs. It had a maximum speed of 255mph, a cruise speed of 185mph, a service ceiling of 25,500ft, and a range of 1,100 miles. The newer and more powerful Helldiver carried a bomb load of up to 2,500lb.

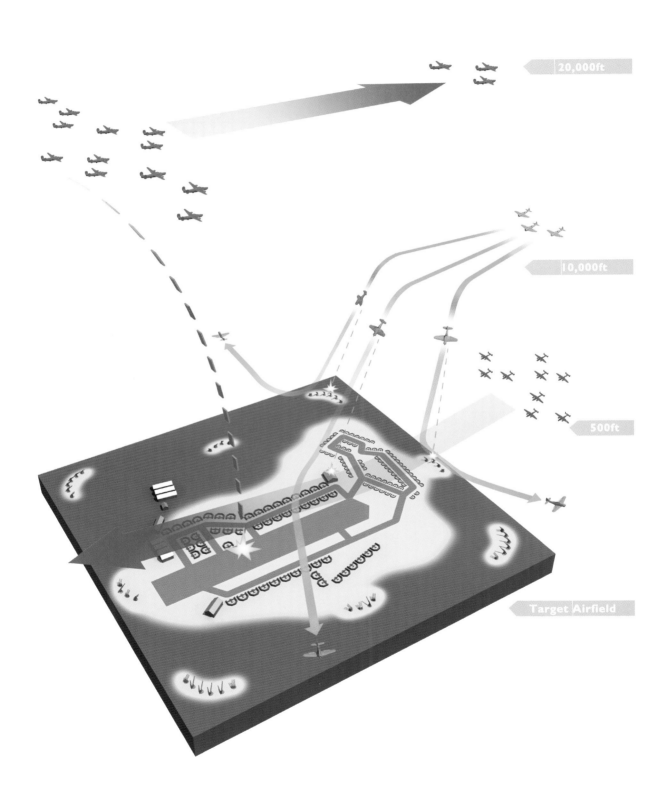

20,000ft

10,000ft

500ft

Target Airfield

OPPOSITE THREE WAYS TO ATTACK AN AIRFIELD

Allied air forces used three basic methods to destroy Japanese airfields: low-level strafing and bombing, high-level bombing, and dive bombing. Each was conducted in a different manner, and had different attributes.

High-level bombing: High-level attacks were made at 20,000ft, near the operational limit of antiaircraft artillery. The bombers flew over the target in a bomber box formation and attempted to saturate the field with a carpet of bombs. Usually flown by B-24s. Advantages: Allowed large numbers of aircraft to simultaneously attack airfield. Flew at or above the ceiling of antiaircraft guns. Box formation offered protection against enemy fighters. Disadvantage: Accuracy diminished by altitude. Many aircraft required.

Dive bombing: Dive bombers attacked in formations of three to six aircraft. They approached at 10,000–12,000ft, picked a specific target, and dived on it at a 70-degree angle, pulling out of the dive at 1,000–2,000ft after releasing their bomb. Typically flown by Douglas Dauntlesses. Advantages: Allowed precision targeting of high-value targets such as antiaircraft gun emplacements. Diving bombers were hard to hit with antiaircraft fire and difficult for fighters to engage. Disadvantages: Dive bombers were often relatively slow and thus vulnerable to fighters and antiaircraft guns prior to entering dives. They also had a shorter range than multi-engine bombers.

Low-level attack: Low-level attacks were made at treetop level by shallow vees of medium bombers, flying under antiaircraft fire. Typically one squadron (12–18 aircraft) attacked at a time, with each wave of aircraft separated by 30 seconds. They strafed their targets, and dropped parachute-retarded time-delay bombs. Typically flown by B-25s. Advantages: Difficult for airfield defenders to attack very low formation. Allowed accurate targeting of targets. Disadvantage: Difficult to launch mass multi-squadron attacks due to risk of trailing aircraft being damaged by bombs from earlier waves.

It had a maximum speed of 295mph, a cruise speed of 158mph, a ceiling of 29,000ft, and a range of 1,165 miles. The Helldiver was a replacement for the Dauntless. At least two carrier-based squadrons were used during the campaign. Two land-based and three carrier-based Navy squadrons used SBDs during the campaign, as well as eight land-based USMC squadrons. The Marine squadrons began replacing Dauntlesses with Helldivers in the last months of the campaign.

Lockheed P-38 Lightning

A twin-engine long-range fighter used by the US Army, it had a maximum speed of 414mph, a cruise speed of 275mph, a 1,300-mile range, and a service ceiling of 44,000ft. It was armed with one 20mm cannon and four .50-caliber machine guns, mounted in the nose. Although

The P-38 could escort bombers from Port Moresby to Rabaul, but flew from airfields at Kiriwina and the Woodlarks. Less maneuverable than the Corsair or Hellcat, properly handled the Lockheed Lightning could match the Japanese fighters. It was the key to the Fifth Air Force's Rabaul offensive. (AC)

vulnerable in a dogfight, its high speed and ceiling allowed the Lightning to pick its battles. It was used exclusively by the USAAF. The Fifth Air Force had six squadrons of P-38s, and committed as many as 70 Lightnings to escort bombers to Rabaul. The Thirteenth Air Force had four P-38 squadrons.

Grumman F6F Hellcat
The successor to Grumman's F4F Wildcat, the Hellcat was designed to give the US Navy a fighter that outmatched the Zero. It first saw combat in September 1943, and was the Allied fighter most feared by Japanese pilots. The Hellcat was armed with six .50-caliber machine guns and had a maximum speed of 391mph, a cruising speed of 200mph, a service ceiling of 37,300ft, and a range of 1,500 miles. It was the primary carrier-based fighter of the war in 1943–44, although it was also used in land-based squadrons. The Navy used four land-based and six carrier-based F6F squadrons against Rabaul.

Vought F4U Corsair
The Corsair was a single-engine fighter, armed with six .50-caliber machine guns. It had a top speed of 417mph, a cruise speed of 215mph, a service ceiling of 36,000ft, and a range of 1,000 miles. It had been designed as a carrier aircraft, but proved difficult to land on an aircraft carrier. In 1943–44 it was assigned to land-based squadrons, although on at least one occasion during this campaign land-based F4Us landed on aircraft carriers to refuel. The Corsair was the dominant fighter of the campaign. The Navy had one squadron of land-based Corsairs and the USMC had 14.

Other aircraft types
The PBY Catalina was an amphibian used for long-range reconnaissance, night antishipping attacks, and air-sea rescue. The USAAF had several squadrons equipped with P-39 Airacobras and P-40 Warhawks. The Airacobra had a 37mm cannon and was used for ground support. The P-40s tended to be used for airfield defense. Since the Japanese made only two airstrikes on Fifth Air Force airfields their role was minimal. The Navy also used the Ventura in a minor role as a patrol bomber.

The RAAF and the Royal New Zealand Air Force (RNZAF) also contributed aircraft used in this campaign. The RAAF had several squadrons of Beaufighters and Beauforts supporting the siege. Both were twin-engine aircraft. The Beaufort was a torpedo bomber, used primarily for night strikes. The Beaufighter was a fighter version of the Beaufort. Intended as a night fighter, it was used to attack airfields. The RNZAF had several Kittyhawk (an export version of the P-40) squadrons stationed in the Solomons. These participated in several fighter sweeps.

The need for bases
Fifth Air Force's success in the March 1943 battle of the Bismarck Sea demonstrated that if the Allies gained air superiority over the Gazelle Peninsula, Rabaul could be effectively isolated without an invasion. But mounting a sustained aerial attack against Rabaul required airfields within range of the target and their associated facilities. It also meant secure supply lines for the airfields and for troops holding the ground around the airfields used.

In January 1943, when Rabaul was made an objective, the nearest available operational airfields to Rabaul were Port Moresby and Guadalcanal. (Dobodura airfield, newly built on the northern coast of New Guinea, was operational, but operations there were still focused exclusively on supplying and protecting Dobodura itself.) Guadalcanal was 650 miles from Rabaul which placed it out of range of all but long-range bombers, unescorted by fighters. Port Moresby was 485 miles from Rabaul, at the ragged edge of the limit for P-38s to

escort Fifth Air Force bombers. Missions from it were complicated by the need to fly over the 13,000ft-high Owen Stanley mountain range shortly after take-off, while heavily laden with bombs and fuel.

By March 1943, when the decision was made to isolate Rabaul purely through air power, facilities had improved, but only marginally. The new airfield at Dobodura was finally operational. Dobodura was only 390 miles from Rabaul, allowing P-38s to reach Rabaul with enough fuel to protect the bombers. Dobodura also eased the challenge of overflying the Owen Stanley Range, as bombers could stage from the new airfield, having topped up their fuel tanks there. From Dobodura the Fifth Air Force was within effective range of Rabaul. Yet the Fifth Air Force had other, nearer enemies at hand, notably at Lae, Finschhafen and Wewak. Japanese air power on New Guinea proved a more immediate threat. Dobodura was ideally placed to deal with these and, as the battle of the Bismarck Sea proved, to sever New Guinea from receiving reinforcements from New Britain.

However, Dobodura was not the ideal platform from which to attack Rabaul. Only multi-engine aircraft could reach the Gazelle Peninsula from there, and the twin-engine P-38 was not a sufficiently agile fighter to be used to wear down the Japanese Zeroes on Rabaul. Single-engine fighters were necessary to gain air superiority, and being able to use land-based dive bombers would give the Allies important precision-bombing capabilities.

The next six months, from April 1943 through mid-October 1943, were therefore devoted to obtaining airfields closer to Rabaul. In April 1943 US Army troops landed on the Woodlark Islands and Kiriwina, lightly held islands where airfields were built. Woodlark was 345 miles from Rabaul while Kiriwina was only 310 miles. In the Solomons, Marines and Army forces began moving up the island chain. In August, Marines landed on New Georgia, seizing the Japanese airfield at Munda, 440 miles from Rabaul. Vella Lavella followed. By late September an airfield there was available. By the start of October the Allies held former Japanese strongpoints in New Guinea, including Lae and Finschhafen.

These landings set the pattern followed in the rest of the campaign. A ring of airfields was built around Rabaul as the campaign progressed by seizing lightly defended existing Japanese airfields or landing where the Japanese were not and building airfields there. Action against heavily contested Japanese positions was limited to New Guinea itself, for reasons independent of the reduction of Rabaul.

The ability of the Allies to quickly build airfields contributed significantly to victory. An airfield could be completed in as little as two weeks. This photo shows an airfield being built. It is Day 8, and the engineers are rolling and grading the runway. (AC)

The United States used aircraft carriers as mobile airfields several times during the campaign, attacking Rabaul and Kavieng. The most critical attack was launched on November 5, 1943. *Saratoga*, pictured here, participated. (USNHHC)

Japanese airfields in western New Britain were being captured. Arawe and Cape Gloucester were taken in December 1943, with their airfields operational for Allied use by January 1944. Gatsama and Talasea, in the middle of New Britain, were snapped up in April. None proved critical in the campaign, but they provided bases from which the Allies could further isolate Rabaul. In 1944 airfields were also built on the Green Islands (160 miles from Rabaul), Emirau (250 miles), and the Admiralties (375 miles). The last two were north of Rabaul. They were occupied as the campaign reached its end, largely to isolate Rabaul by completing the ring of airfields around the fortress.

Lastly, aircraft carriers provided further, mobile airfields around Rabaul. In early 1943, the United States had only one prewar fleet carrier, *Saratoga*, available. By fall, new construction was replacing the prewar carriers lost in 1942. In addition, two new Essex-class fleet carriers, *Essex* and *Bunker Hill*, and three light carriers (built on cruiser hulls), *Princeton*, *Independence*, and *Monterey*, were used to strike Rabaul or Kavieng. Carrier aircraft could hit targets up to 250 miles away, allowing for necessary reserves.

Balanced against that was the fact that aircraft carriers were extremely vulnerable to airstrikes when without fighter cover. A strike against Rabaul, especially during the period when it still had fighter protection, required commitment of the entire carrier air group, including fighters. The Navy made three carrier strikes against Rabaul, and two on Kavieng. These targeted Japanese ships, but provided a critical injection of airpower at a decisive moment.

Backing all of this was a logistical chain which ran from the West Coast to New Guinea. Every aircraft, bullet, bomb, and gallon of fuel had to be brought across the Pacific and guarded from enemy attack once in the war zone. The United States built a logistical chain which provided the Allies with the weapons and supplies they needed, as needed. Apart from occasional shortages of aircraft and warships, the assets in theater always had sufficient logistics.

Weapons and tactics

The aerial forces of the United States and its allies were relatively ineffective during 1942, despite their strategic successes. Several major naval victories were won through dive bombing, and US fighters, especially Navy and Marine Corps aircraft, proved effective in defense, particularly when radar was available to direct aircraft to the enemy. But medium-altitude bombing of both ships and airfields had been unproductive, especially by USAAF units. In early 1943 new weapons and tactics were introduced.

One of the most radical changes was in bombing doctrine. New bombing techniques were developed by the Fifth Air Force, spearheaded by its leader George Kenney. Kenney pioneered low-level attack, using two new techniques.

The first was skip bombing. This involved making a mast-top pass at a target ship, flying the length of a fleeing ship. Bombs were dropped as the bomber approached. If the bomb landed on the ship, it would explode, causing damage. Bombs which missed skipped along the ship's side, exploding next to the ship, staving in the sides above and below the waterline. Kenney personally demonstrated skip bombing in an experiment in Fiji, in July 1942. That fall he had several Fifth Air Force bomb groups practicing the technique, using a wrecked ship outside Port Moresby as a training target.

This low-level technique reduced the need for a bombardier, as the pilot dropped the bombs. One of Kenney's group commanders, Paul Gunn, was converting A-20 light bombers into strafers, adding four .50-caliber machine guns in the nose, in the bombardier's position. Kenney had Gunn make this field modification to a squadron of B-25s, augmenting the four .50-caliber guns in the nose with four additional guns added in pods to the sides of the bomber – two on each side attached below the pilot's seat.

The .50-caliber was extremely powerful for a machine gun, especially against unarmored targets such as cargo ships. A bullet could penetrate a cargo ship's deck and hull plating, and punch holes through the ship's engines. It fired 450–600 rounds per minute. A ten-second strafing pass let a modified B-25 hit a targeted ship with 600–800 rounds. Additionally the modification allowed the bomber to keep its bomb load. The B-25 became the deadliest antiship weapon in the Southwest Pacific. Soon every B-25 in the Fifth Air Force was modified into a gunship, as were most of the B-25s in Thirteenth Air Force, Marine, and Navy squadrons operating out of the Solomons.

General George Kenney led the Fifth Air Force. A brilliant tactician, he pioneered techniques that permitted the USAAF to devastate Japanese sea and air power. (AC)

1: B-25 spots ship, turns towards ship and dives

2: Ship spots B-25, turns away from B-25 fearing a torpedo attack

3: B-25 begins firing machine guns to suppress AA and damage ship

4: One dropped bomb hits ship, the second explodes next to it. B-25 pulls up and out

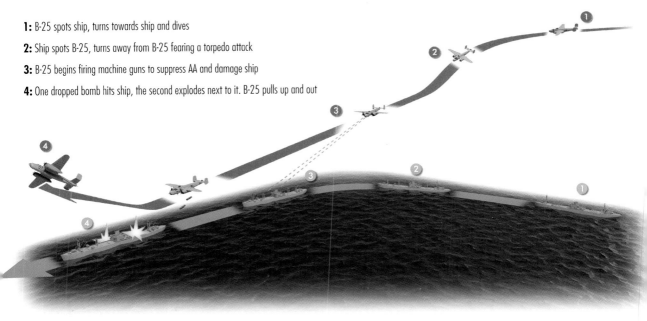

ABOVE SKIP BOMBING: HOW TO DO IT

Until skip bombing was developed Army bombers had a dismal record when attacking naval targets. Skip bombers came in low (at mast-top heights) flying the length of the ship they were targeting. If the bomb fell short or long of the aim point (typically the ship's funnel) it was more likely to hit the ship than if the attack were made broadside. If it missed left or right, it would explode next to the ship, often underwater, rupturing the hull. Bombers, typically equipped with eight forward-firing .50-caliber machine guns, would rake the ship with bullets capable of penetrating a destroyer's turret or piercing completely through the hull of a cargo ship.

Parachute-delayed fragmentation bombs are dropped on Lakunai. This allowed low-level bombers to destroy enemy aircraft on the ground without being destroyed by their own bombs. (USNHHC)

Kenney also pioneered new ordnance types. One was the daisy-cutter, a conventional 300lb or 500lb bomb wrapped with ¼in-diameter steel wire. It was fitted with a contact fuse attached to the end of the bomb by a 6in pipe. The bomb exploded at waist height. The wire fractured into pieces between 6in and 2ft long, spraying pieces in all directions. A daisy-cutter flattened everything within 100ft, and shredded aircraft within 100 yards of the impact point. The wire flew through the air with a whistling noise, terrifying and demoralizing men who had previously witnessed its effects on their comrades. As with the gun B-25s, daisy-cutters were a field modification, developed in theater by the Fifth Air Force.

While the daisy-cutter was an effective weapon for destroying aircraft on the ground, due to its instantaneous fuse, it was difficult to use in low-level missions. There Kenney relied on two different types of ordnance, the para-frag and the phosphorus bomb.

The para-frag bomb was a 10kg (23lb) fragmentation bomb with a parachute attached. The bombs had contact fuses, but the parachute slowed the bomb's descent, allowing up to 90 seconds between the time the bomb was dropped and the time it struck the ground and exploded. This allowed low-level bombers to conduct a strafing pass on an airfield, drop the bombs while flying over the target, and be beyond the target area when the bombs detonated. Para-frags were carried in clusters of three with a B-25 typically carrying 12 clusters. The Allies also made use of phosphorus bombs against airfields and the supply facilities around Rabaul. The white phosphorus bombs worked both as incendiaries, for starting fires, and to create smokescreens limiting the defenders' visibility. Much of the city of Rabaul was destroyed through firebombing.

When making low-level attacks against airfields an entire squadron of 12–16 aircraft, typically B-25s, would attack in line abreast. If multiple squadrons attacked the same airfield, each squadron attacked individually, with the waves of aircraft spaced 90 seconds to three minutes apart to ensure no Allied aircraft were destroyed by fratricide.

The Fifth Air Force also used phosphorus bombs against Japanese aircraft on the ground. A strike camera photo shows the phosphorus bombs exploding over Lakunai airfield during a November 1943 raid. Two G4Ms and an A6M fighter are targeted. (USAAF)

DEFENDERS' CAPABILITIES
Fortress Rabaul

Doctrine

By the start of 1943, Japan had changed war objectives twice. Its original objective had been to conquer enough territory to supply Japan with its strategic needs – petroleum, rubber, food, and metals – within a defensible perimeter. The resources were located in the Dutch East Indies (petroleum and rubber) and Indochina (food). The defensive perimeter ran in an arc from Burma along the southern islands of the Dutch East Indies, New Guinea north of the Owen Stanley Range, New Britain and New Ireland, and through the coral atolls of the Central Pacific. Once this perimeter was secured it would be fortified. Japan would wait within it until its enemies wore themselves out attacking it, wearied of war, and negotiated a peace favorable to Japan.

Japan's initial success led to informal revision of that objective. Instead of establishing a defensive perimeter along that line, victory encouraged them to expand the perimeter beyond the original limits. The Solomon Islands, Aleutians, and Midway were added. The offensive in New Guinea was expanded to include the southern half of the island. Japan even briefly considered invading Australia. Instead of waiting for the Allies to tire of attacking a fortified defensive perimeter, Japan would keep pushing the enemy back until it sued for peace.

That decision led to disaster. Between May 1942 and January 1943 Japan experienced a series of severe setbacks as a result of expansion beyond its original perimeter. This included the loss of four fleet carriers at Midway, and a long unsuccessful battle to hold Guadalcanal. By January 1943, Japan had reverted to its original objective of fortifying a defensive perimeter and holding it until the Allies wore themselves out attacking.

For Southeast Area, holding Rabaul and the north coast of New Guinea was critical. To Japan they seemed the keystones in their defensive arc. Without them, especially Rabaul, the arc would crumble. The Allies were on the advance in New Guinea, threatening Japan's

The Mitsubishi A6M3 was a mid-war version of the Zero, distinguishable by its squared wingtips. Despite its more robust construction many Japanese pilots preferred the older but more maneuverable A6M2. Allied intelligence believed it was a new fighter, codenaming it Hap or Hamp. (AC)

Vice Admiral Jinichi Kusaka was the senior naval officer in the Southeast Area. Once Imperial Japanese Army aircraft departed to New Guinea, Kusaka commanded the only aircraft operating out of Rabaul. He held primary responsibility for Rabaul's air defense during the Allied air offensive. (USNHHC)

defensive perimeter. They were also advancing up the Solomons, but these islands – except possibly Bougainville – fell outside Japan's defensive ring. Imperial Headquarters chose to pursue a policy of active defense in the Solomons and aggressive offensive in New Guinea in 1943. This resulted in a drawdown of Army assets in Rabaul, especially aircraft, as resources were transferred to New Guinea. By October, virtually all Imperial Japanese Army aircraft had left Rabaul, and its aerial defense would be conducted almost exclusively by the Navy, principally the land-based Eleventh Air Fleet, assisted by the Eighth Fleet, based at Rabaul. Japanese plans for defending Rabaul consisted of keeping Allied forces as far from Rabaul as possible through a stubborn defense of the southern islands of the Solomon chain. To that end, the Japanese Navy attempted two air offensives in 1943: Operation *I* and Operation *RO*. Both were intended as crushing air operations, which would sweep Allied forces south.

Operation *I* took place in April 1943. The air contingents of four Japanese aircraft carriers and the remaining G3M and G4M "*rikko*" bomber squadrons were sent to Rabaul. Combined with the air fleet at Rabaul, this brought a force of over 350 aircraft to attack the United States at the just-taken Russell Islands. It was the largest concentration of Japanese airpower since Pearl Harbor. Japan hoped for a similar result: one or two massive airstrikes which would cripple the target. Instead the operation resulted in heavy aircraft losses by the Japanese, minor losses for the United States, and the death of Isoroku Yamamoto, Japan's ablest admiral.

Operation *RO*, originally scheduled for September 1943, was delayed until October. It reprised Operation *I*. Again, the carrier aircraft from the Combined Fleet were sent to Rabaul with the intention of launching a single massive strike against the Allies, reversing the momentum of the Allied offensive. Operation *RO* became entangled in the Allied air offensive against Rabaul, which started before *RO* began.

Both operations highlighted the weakness of Japanese air doctrine and strategy. Both were based on a belief that a few but massive airstrikes would change the balance in a theater. This worked in the opening months of the war. Pearl Harbor crippled the US Navy. Japan gained air superiority over the Philippines with a few days' bombing of Clark Field and other American airfields in Luzon. The Indian Ocean Raid of March 31–April 10, 1943 had chased the Royal Navy out of the Bay of Bengal and the western Indian Ocean.

It had worked because those attacks were made against foes that were surprised or lacking reserves. By 1943, however, the Allies were practiced in meeting air raids, and had enough aircraft to meet even massive Japanese air raids on equal terms and replace losses incurred. Since defeat was unthinkable, Japan kept using its previous strategy of bold decisive strikes to overwhelm the foe. It was a triumph of hope over experience.

Faulty Japanese intelligence was another weakness. Excessive assessment of damage to enemy forces was routinely accepted. Attacks were prematurely discontinued because objectives had seemingly been achieved. Since the reported number of ships sunk or aircraft downed often exceeded what the opposition was estimated to have, further operations were thought unnecessary.

Japan knew that it could not win a war of attrition, but it was forced into one at Rabaul. Throughout 1943 aircrew were lost at rates higher than Japan could replace them. In part this was due to Japan's exacting training standards. Competent trainees who were not brilliant performers were washed out – a practice which continued after the war started. This left Japan without men to fly the aircraft available.

By 1943 it was apparent to Japan that it could not win a quick victory, and was incapable of winning an attrition battle. At Rabaul Japan's strategy was simply to refuse to concede the possibility of defeat and keep throwing inadequate numbers of fighters at an ever-increasing number of attacking bombers and fighter aircraft. Japan achieved its objective of holding Rabaul, but only at the sufferance of its opponents and to the detriment of its efforts elsewhere.

The Japanese capability to defend Rabaul depended on the same three factors as the Allies: aircraft, facilities, and weapons and tactics. Rabaul was jointly defended by the Imperial Japanese Navy and the Imperial Japanese Army. These two services cooperated closely, if not always gladly, at Rabaul. The Emperor ordered cooperation, and in Imperial Japan the Emperor's command was literally the word of God. Despite losses in 1942, formidable capabilities remained to the Japanese at the start of the campaign.

The two services conducted a joint air defense of Rabaul through much of 1942 and 1943 with both Army and Navy aircraft patrolling the skies over the Gazelle Peninsula. Aircraft losses in New Guinea in August and September 1943 forced realignment. To make up the shortfall in New Guinea, Army aircraft in New Britain were transferred to New Guinea. Sending one service simplified supply, and the shorter-ranged Army aircraft were more useful on New Guinea. The Army continued to play an important role in the air defense of Rabaul as it operated over half of Rabaul's antiaircraft guns.

Japanese defensive capabilities were bolstered by generous stocks of fuel, food, ammunition, and supplies. Rabaul was to be the supply depot for the future Japanese expansion which never occurred, and so throughout 1942 these supplies had poured in. They were available for its defense. Rabaul was the most heavily defended Japanese citadel in the Southwest Pacific and one of the most heavily defended in the Pacific. But Japan's biggest weakness was its lack of replacements, in aircraft, pilots, and supplies. It had to fight with what was on hand.

Admiral Mineichi Koga commanded the Japanese Combined Fleet stationed at Truk during the siege of Rabaul. In that role he could send aircraft and warships to reinforce Rabaul's permanent garrison. (USNHHC)

Aircraft

The Japanese had nearly 300 land-based aircraft stationed on Rabaul when the Allied campaign to reduce Rabaul began. Up to 300 additional carrier aircraft from the Combined Fleet were available. These reserve aircraft, normally at Truk, were shuttled in as needed. Six types of aircraft defended Rabaul. These included:

Mitsubishi A6M ("Zero," "Zeke," "Hamp")

This was the famous (or infamous to the Allies) Mitsubishi *Reisen* (Zero). The Zero dominated the Pacific in 1941 and 1942, so much so that the Imperial Japanese Navy delayed developing a replacement. By 1943 it was becoming outclassed by new Allied fighters, especially the F6F and F4U. Two types of Zeroes were used at Rabaul, the A6M2 (called "Zeke" by the Allies) and A6M3 (Hap or Hamp). Both types were armed with two 7.7mm machine guns and two 20mm cannon (Type 99-1 for A6M2 and Type 99-2 for A6M3). Both versions had a service ceiling of 32,000ft and a top speed of 332mph. The A6M2 had a range of 1,600 miles. The A6M3 had a shorter range, but was still capable of ferrying from Truk to Rabaul and of providing airfield defense. Although the A6M3 had a more powerful cannon and better protection, Rabaul pilots preferred the older A6M2 due to its greater maneuverability. There were 150 A6Ms stationed at Rabaul at the start of the campaign. These were frequently reinforced by carrier force aircraft.

Mitsubishi G3M ("Nell") and G4M ("Betty")

These were two twin-engine bombers developed as long-range bombers for the Imperial Japanese Navy. These land-based attack (*rikko*) bombers were intended to offset Japanese naval treaty tonnage limitations by substituting aircraft for warships. They were effective ship-killers early in the war, especially the G4M. Both carried one aerial torpedo or up to 800kg (1,760lb) of bombs. The G3M had a top speed of 233mph, a cruising speed of 174mph, and a range of 2,700 miles. The G4M had a top speed of 365mph, a cruising speed of 196mph, and a range of 1,770 miles. There were 87 G3Ms and G4Ms (mostly G4Ms) at Rabaul at the beginning of October. Many were destroyed on the ground at the outset of the campaign and they played a minor role thereafter.

G4M bombers in revetments at Vunakanau Airfield near Rabaul. The Mitsubishi G4M (Betty) formed the backbone of Japan's long-range land-based *rikko* squadrons. This photo was taken by photo reconnaissance aircraft prior to the Fifth Air Force's airstrikes in October, 1943. (USAAF)

Yokosuka D4Y1 ("Judy")

The D4Y1 was intended as a dive bomber, a replacement for the Aichi D3A. The airplane proved to have structural problems. Unable to serve as a dive bomber, it was used for reconnaissance and as a level bomber. It was fast (a 342mph maximum speed) with a range of 910 miles and a 35,000ft service ceiling. It was armed with two forward-firing 7.7mm machine guns and one rearward-firing flexible 7.7mm machine gun, and could carry 1,000lb of bombs. One of the few Japanese aircraft with an inline liquid-cooled engine, it was often mistaken for the Kawasaki Ki-61 ("Tony"), an Army fighter. The confusion was compounded because D4Y1s were used for air defense at Rabaul. Armed with small time-fused bombs intended to explode mid-air, it flew over Allied bomber formations dropping air-to-air bombs in the hope of breaking up formations. One air group with 20 D4Y1s was stationed at Rabaul.

The Yokosuka D4Y1 (Judy) was intended to replace the Aichi D3A (Val) dive bomber. Structural issues prevented its use in dive bombing. At Rabaul its primary use was dropping air-burst phosphorous bombs on Allied bomber formations – an almost totally ineffective tactic. (AC)

Nakajima B5N ("Kate")

The B5N was the standard carrier-based torpedo bomber for the Imperial Japanese Navy during World War II. It carried one 800kg (1,760lb) aerial torpedo, or up to 800kg in bombs, with a maximum speed of 235mph, a cruising speed of 161mph, a ceiling of 27,000ft, and a range of 1,200 miles. During the Rabaul campaign, the B5N was the primary threat to US Navy carriers attacking Rabaul. Japanese aerial torpedoes were deadly – faster, longer-ranged, with a larger warhead, and mechanically more reliable than Allied aerial torpedoes. The threat was mitigated because at the start of the campaign only 12 B5Ns were stationed at Rabaul, although Combined Fleet B5Ns could and were staged in to Rabaul at different times during the campaign.

Aichi D3A ("Val")

A monoplane with fixed landing gear, the D3A was Japan's standard dive bomber through most of the war. It was more a contemporary of the German Ju 87 Stuka than of the United States' Dauntless and Helldiver dive bombers. It was to have been replaced by 1943, but problems with the D4Y1 kept the D3A in service. It had a top speed of 267mph, a cruising speed of 184mph, a ceiling of 34,500ft, and a range of 840 miles. It could carry one 250kg (551lb) bomb, making it significantly weaker than any other Pacific Theater dive bomber. Twenty-four D3As were stationed at Rabaul in the same air group as the B5Ns. As with the B5Ns, additional D3As could be staged to Rabaul, although with their shorter range, they generally staged through Kavieng.

All Japanese aircraft suffered an inability to take damage. In the search for the maximum possible range and attack capability anything viewed as unnecessary weight was omitted. This included armor protecting the crew and vital components, self-sealing gas tanks, and even radios. Only element leaders had radios. Japanese aircraft were vulnerable to the .50-caliber machine guns of US aircraft, and caught fire easily. (The Japanese called the G4M the "Type 1 Cigarette Lighter.") The lack of radios made it difficult to control fighters in the air, as communications were limited to hand signals. By contrast, when US Navy aircraft attacked Simpson Harbor on November 5, 1943, the attack plan was developed in flight by discussion among the attacking aircrew.

Airfields and infrastructure

By October 1943 Japan had four operational airfields in the Gazelle Peninsula to protect Rabaul and Simpson Harbor, and a non-operational fifth airfield on the peninsula available if needed. Two airfields, Lakunai and Vunakanau, existed when the Japanese captured Rabaul. Both then had grass runways. The Japanese improved both airfields. Lakunai was given a 4,300ft by 650ft runway topped with sand and crushed coral. Two and a half miles of taxiways, 90 fighter revetments and ten bomber revetments, and support buildings were added. Vunakanau received even greater improvements. A graded landing strip 5,200ft by 720ft included a concrete-paved center section 4,200ft by 175ft. Vunakanau had 90 fighter and 60 bomber revetments linked by 5½ miles of taxiways.

Rapopo, 14 miles southeast of Rabaul, Keravat, 13 miles southwest of Rabaul, and Tobera, 20 miles south of Rabaul and deep in the jungle of the Gazelle Peninsula, were added in 1942–43. Rapopo and Tobera were given concrete runways – 4,600 by 630ft for Rapopo and 3,600 by 100ft for Tobera. (Tobera's concrete strip lay in a 4,800 by 400ft graded surface.) Keravat had a 4,250 by 300ft graded surface, but was not paved or further improved due to drainage problems. It was used as a backup landing field. Rapopo was intended as an Army bomber base, with 90 bomber and ten fighter revetments. Tobera was a fighter strip, with revetments for 75 fighters and two bombers.

OPPOSITE THE NORTHEASTERN GAZELLE PENINSULA

This constellation of airfields gave the Japanese strategic depth. If one were temporarily knocked out, aircraft could operate out of the remaining fields. To suppress Rabaul the Allies had to reduce all four operational airstrips, a challenging task, one the Japanese felt insurmountable.

The Japanese also had a network of airfields around New Britain, New Ireland, and the northern Solomons to provide defense in depth. Most were grass strips with light garrisons. As the campaign progressed some proved to be liabilities. They were seized by Allied forces, with the airfields turned against their original owners. The airfields on Bougainville and New Ireland were heavily garrisoned. Their units had to be subdued before Rabaul could be approached from that direction.

Antiaircraft defenses

Aircraft were not the only resource protecting Rabaul from air attack. Japan invested much of its available air warning radar defending Rabaul. The Imperial Japanese Navy built 30 fixed early warning radar sets during World War II. Eleven were sent to defend Rabaul. Seven were on New Britain, scattered around the Gazelle Peninsula. Four were on New Ireland. These could detect formations of aircraft 250km (150 miles) distant and single aircraft at up to 100km (62 miles) distance. Twenty-two Type 6 Aircraft radars were also sent to Rabaul, and removed for conversion to ground-based tracking units. Half were installed, seven on New Ireland and four on New Britain. These could detect formations at 100km (62 miles) and single aircraft at 70km (43 miles).

The Gazelle Peninsula was well equipped with antiaircraft artillery. The Army had 72 3in or 75mm guns and 120 20mm antiaircraft/antitank or 13.2mm machine guns stationed near Rabaul; the Navy had eight 12.7cm and 15 12cm dual-purpose guns, 23 3in or 75mm guns, 92 25mm antiaircraft guns and 37 machine guns ringing Blanche Bay and

Lakunai was one of two RAAF fields taken over by the Japanese when they occupied Rabaul. It had a crushed-coral runway. It was primarily used as a fighter strip by the Imperial Japanese Navy. (AC)

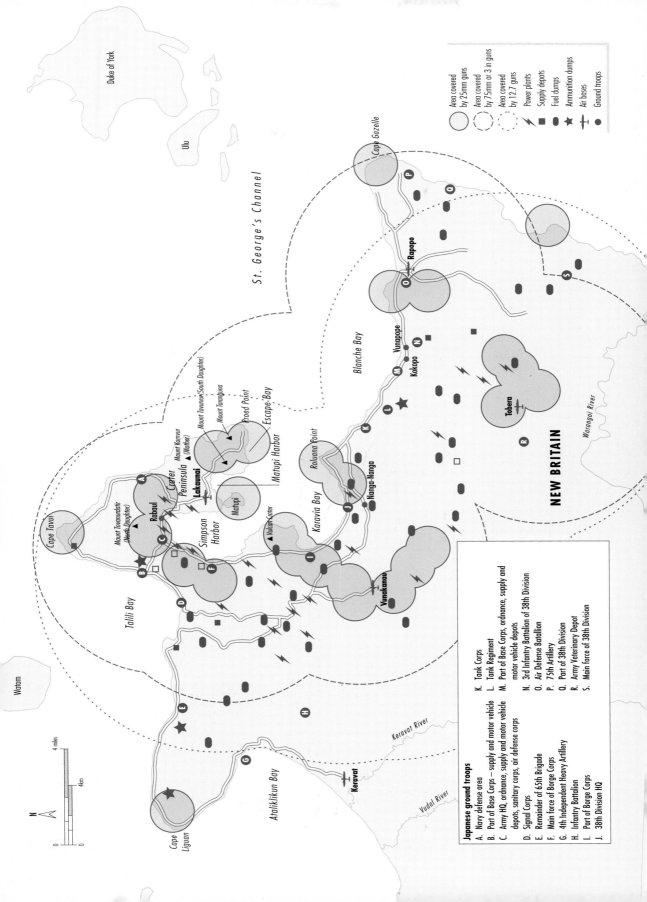

N

0   4 miles
0   4km

Watom

Duke of York

Ulu

St. George's Channel

Ataliklikun Bay

Talili Bay

Cape Liguan

Cape Tavui

Keravat River

Vudal River

Keravat

Keravat River

Rabaul

Mount Tovaurdahir (North Daughter)

Mount Tovanvur (South Daughter)

Mount Tavurvuru

Crater Peninsula

Mount Kamur (Mother)

Mount Tarangua

Lakunai

Praed Point

Escape Bay

Matupi Harbor

Matupi

Simpson Harbor

Vulcan Crater

Karavia Bay

Roluana Point

Vunakanau

Nanga-Nanga

Kokopo

Vunapope

Blanche Bay

Rapopo

Cape Gazelle

Tobera

Warangoi River

NEW BRITAIN

A
B
C
D
E
F
G
H
I
J
K
L
M
N
O
P
Q
R
S

Japanese ground troops

A. Navy defense area
B. Part of Base Corps – supply and motor vehicle
C. Army HQ, ordnance, supply and motor vehicle depots, sanitary corps, air defense corps
D. Signal Corps
E. Remainder of 65th Brigade
F. Main force of Borge Corps
G. 4th Independent Heavy Artillery
H. Infantry Battalion
I. Part of Borge Corps
J. 38th Division HQ

K. Tank Corps
L. Tank Regiment
M. Part of Base Corps, ordnance, supply and motor vehicle depots
N. 3rd Infantry Battalion of 38th Division
O. Air Defense Battalion
P. 75th Artillery
Q. Part of 38th Division
R. Army Veterinary Depot
S. Main force of 38th Division

Area covered by 25mm guns

Area covered by 75mm or 3 in guns

Area covered by 12.7 guns

Power plants
Supply depots
Fuel dumps
Ammunition dumps
Air bases
Ground troops

Keravat Airfield was never finished due to drainage problems. It was available as an emergency strip or as a backup strip when necessary. (AC)

Simpson Harbor or protecting their airfields. Heavy concentrations of antiaircraft artillery protected Kavieng on the northern end of New Ireland and St George Point on its southern tip. While there was no airfield at St George Point, a radar complex there provided early warning of aircraft inbound from the Solomons.

Since Rabaul was the headquarters and main supply base for both the Southeastern Army Forces and the Southeastern Fleet, it had some of the largest supply bases in the Southwest Pacific. At the start of the Allied campaign against Rabaul it was well stocked with food, supplies, munitions, and fuel. The Gazelle Peninsula was filled with warehouses stuffed with supplies, linked by a road network with 500 miles of improved roads. Eighty percent were built after Japan occupied Rabaul.

The Army had 30,000 tons of ammunition stockpiled. Much was intended for the use of the 100,000-plus ground forces they had in the Gazelle Peninsula, but included generous stocks of antiaircraft artillery ammunition. The Japanese Navy had over 1.5 million rounds of antiaircraft ammunition, for everything from its 12.7cm heavy antiaircraft guns down to 25mm auto-cannon. This was sufficient to supply Japan's air defense needs for many months.

Rabaul's supply dumps held over 55,000 tons of food, 5,400 tons of clothing, 5,000 tons of canteen supplies, 3,300 tons of medical supplies, nearly 6 million gallons of aviation fuel, 1.5 million gallons of motor gasoline and diesel, and 12 million gallons of lubricants and other petroleum products. There were nearly 5,000 motor vehicles on the Gazelle Peninsula. Enough was stockpiled to feed the garrison for nearly a year at full rations, and allow every fighter stationed at Rabaul to fly at least 300 times. The Allies could not starve the Japanese out.

None of these stores were adequately protected in October 1943, however. Fuel was in above-ground bulk storage tanks. Ammunition was in open dumps protected only by earth revetments. Everything else was stored in lightly built wood warehouses, mostly scattered around Blanche Bay and Simpson Harbor. All of it was vulnerable to air attack. Not until 1944, well after the Allied air offensive began, did the Japanese disperse their stores into underground storage facilities.

Weapons and tactics

Japan was faced with a defensive struggle at Rabaul, something for which it was ill-equipped and doctrinally ill-prepared. The Japanese air forces, both naval and army, were instruments of attack, not defense. If you hit your foe first, hit your foe hard, you did not have to defend. Japanese aircraft were optimized for attack; built for long range, maximum bomb load, and maneuverability. It was a strategy which served the Japanese well during the first months of the war – until it did not. Losses at Coral Sea, Midway, and the struggle for Guadalcanal highlighted Japanese weaknesses: vulnerability to attack and inadequate reserves, particularly aircraft and aircrew.

When the Allies started their offensive against Rabaul Japanese weaknesses had become obvious. After their first operations against the encircling Allies, the Japanese on Rabaul ran

The Imperial Japanese Navy sent nearly one-third of its long-range land-based early warning radar units to defend Rabaul. This unit was one of two installed at Tomavatur Mission, 2 miles southeast of Vunakanau. (AC)

out of bombers in the first half of 1943. With only a handful of replacements, counterstrikes against Allied airbases and naval vessels were thereafter rare. The last major Japanese raids against Allied airfields occurred in mid-October, while the last attempts to attack either an invasion fleet or a US Navy carrier task force were made in November. From then on, the Japanese defense of Rabaul depended solely on its fighter aircraft, bombers attacking aerial targets, and antiaircraft artillery. This ceded the initiative to the Allies, who thereafter set the tempo of their air offensive.

While Japan had radar at Rabaul, it never developed an integrated air defense system to take advantage of radar's capabilities. Radar only provided an alert of impending raids. It was a glorified and long-range coast-watcher system, like having ground-based observers with 50-mile vision. When an incoming Allied raid was detected the radar sites notified the airfields of the direction and presumed size of the raid. Aircraft were launched and antiaircraft artillery manned based on the expected arrival time and direction. Beyond providing aircraft with a rough vector for the incoming foe, no further guidance was provided once Japanese aircraft were airborne. There was no vectoring or battle control. Fire-control radar did not exist. One attempt to direct fire from one twin-mount 12.7cm antiaircraft gun failed to produce satisfactory results, despite an extended trial period. The experiment was discontinued and the radar unit was dismantled.

Exacerbating the lack of radar vectoring was the inability to coordinate mass formations of fighters. As previously mentioned the aircraft of formation leaders had radios. Once airborne, the other aircraft depended upon hand signals and wing-waggling for communications. This made it difficult to arrange a massed attack on a bomber formation. Instead, individual elements attacked at the formation leader's discretion. Pilots attacked the easiest target rather than the most significant. Stragglers were pursued while a tight formation was bypassed until easier opportunities were disposed of.

The pilots were not afraid to fight. They often displayed almost foolhardy aggressiveness. Some pilots even rammed enemy aircraft rather than let them escape. Rather the problem was that they fought as individual warriors, not as an integrated team. It reduced effectiveness when they could least afford it.

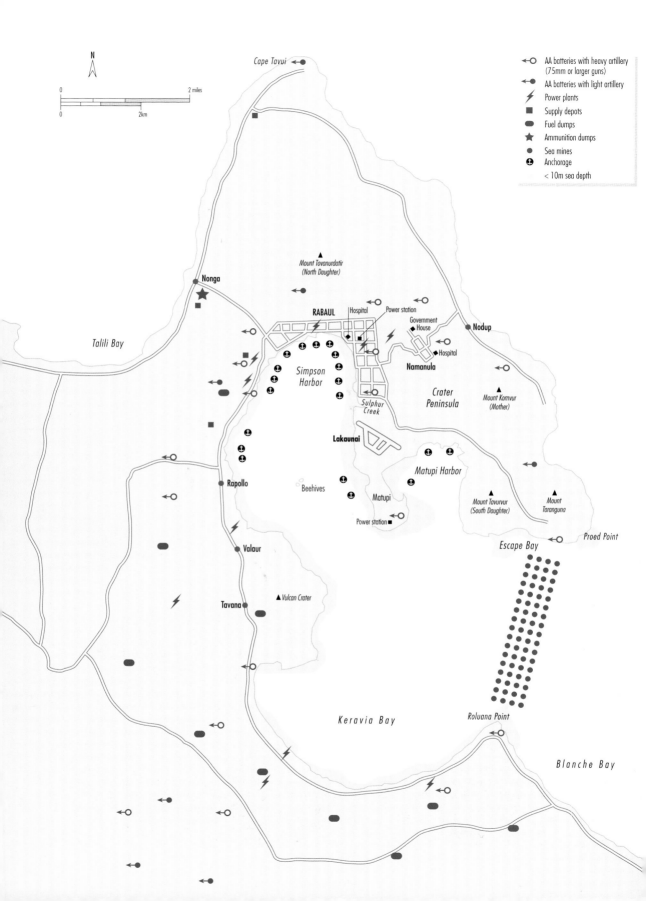

N

0   2 miles
0   2km

AA batteries with heavy artillery
(75mm or larger guns)
AA batteries with light artillery
Power plants
Supply depots
Fuel dumps
Ammunition dumps
Sea mines
Anchorage
< 10m sea depth

Cape Tavui

*Mount Tovanurdatir
(North Daughter)*

Nonga

Talili Bay

RABAUL   Hospital   Power station
Government
House
Nodup

*Simpson
Harbor*

Hospital

Namanula

*Crater
Peninsula*

*Sulphur
Creek*

*Mount Komvur
(Mother)*

Lakaunai

Matupi Harbor

Rapollo

Beehives

Matupi

*Mount Tavurvur
(South Daughter)*

*Mount
Taranguna*

Power station

Valaur

Escape Bay

Proed Point

▲ *Vulcan Crater*

Tavana

Keravia Bay

Roluana Point

Blanche Bay

OPPOSITE RABAUL AND SIMPSON HARBOR

A final antiaircraft weapon wielded by the Japanese was the antiaircraft bomb. When warned of a raid, D4Ys were armed with 30kg and 60kg (66lb and 122lb) aerial phosphorus bombs. The D4Y would fly over a formation of bombers and drop the bomb on the formation. The bombs were time-fused, and – assuming the attacking D4Y was at the correct height above the formation – would explode in the middle of the formation. In theory, the exploding bombs would cause the formation to scatter, or even hit and set fire to a bomber. In practice, they had almost no effect. They rarely damaged Allied bombers, and the bombs' spectacular pyrotechnics even more rarely caused any reaction in a high-altitude formation. The main result of these efforts was to give Allied fighter pilots an opportunity to shoot down a D4Y, thinking it the inline-engine Ki-61 fighter.

While Japan had a lot of antiaircraft artillery on Rabaul, flak never caused serious casualties to Allied attackers. The heaviest Japanese antiaircraft artillery, the 12.7cm and 12cm, had a theoretical effective ceiling of 25,000ft. During the siege of Rabaul they rarely achieved hits on aircraft higher than 20,000ft. The Model 88 75mm antiaircraft gun had an effective ceiling of 21,000ft, and the Model 10 3in gun was effective only up to 18,000ft.

Of the medium antiaircraft artillery, the 25mm machine cannon could hit targets at up to 6,000ft. These were effective guns against targets within their range. The 20mm cannon and 13.2mm machine gun had virtually identical effective ranges, about 3,500ft, but the 20mm was more dangerous because its rounds were both heavier and explosive. These guns were effective if an enemy aircraft attacked at altitudes of between 1,000 and 4,000ft, but the Allies rarely obliged. Aircraft approached targets at medium to high altitudes of 10,000–25,000ft or at treetop level – between 100 and 300ft above the ground. Altitudes of 10,000–25,000ft were above the ceiling of this artillery. At treetop altitudes medium and light antiaircraft had only a very short time window in which to engage. An aircraft traveling at 300mph would fly through the effective range of a 25mm gun in 24 seconds or a 20mm cannon or 13.2mm machine gun in 15 seconds, during which the angle of fire changed rapidly.

One of the 92 25mm antiaircraft guns at Rabaul. This twin-mount 25mm was at Praed Point at the northern tip of the Crater Peninsula. A 25mm gun had an effective altitude of 6,000ft. (AC)

CAMPAIGN OBJECTIVES
Isolating a fortress

The A6M Zero dominated the first 20 months of the Pacific War. By the time the Allies were preparing to knock out Rabaul, it was past its prime, especially the A6M2, shown here. (AC)

By late 1942 Rabaul had become Japan's major air and naval base in the Allied Southwest Pacific Area and the Japanese Southeast Area. Rabaul as a center for Japanese naval and air activity threatened communications with Australia. Before the Allies could advance beyond Rabaul it had to be neutralized. The Allies began planning to retake Rabaul almost as soon as the Japanese captured it.

In January 1942 Admiral Chester Nimitz, commanding naval forces in the Pacific, wanted to take the offensive at the earliest possible opportunity. Carrier raids were made against island outposts held by the Japanese at the fringes of their ocean empire in February 1942. Nimitz also deployed carrier forces in the Southwest Pacific Area as early as March 1942. US carriers stopped the Japanese from capturing Port Moresby, and materially assisted the Allied advance in the Solomons.

Nor was the desire to go on the offensive limited to the US Navy. Chased out of the Philippines, General Douglas MacArthur vowed to return. Headquartered in Australia, and commanding Allied forces in the region, he began offensive actions against the Japanese in late 1942.

MacArthur and Nimitz led the two major commands in the Pacific. Nimitz commanded the Pacific Ocean Areas, divided into the North Pacific Area (everything north of the 42nd parallel), the Central Pacific Area (between the equator and 42 degrees north, except for the area around the Philippines), and the South Pacific Area (everything south of the equator and east of latitude 159 east). MacArthur controlled the Southwest Pacific Area, which included Australia, New Guinea, the Dutch East Indies east of Sumatra, the Philippines and the waters around them. East of New Guinea the northern boundary ran along the equator to 159 degrees east. New Britain, New Ireland, and Rabaul fell within the boundaries of the Southwest Pacific Area, with the Solomons split between the South Pacific Area and the Southwest Pacific Area.

Nimitz assigned a deputy to run the South Pacific Area. By 1943, Admiral William Halsey, an aggressive leader, who revitalized the stalled US effort to secure Guadalcanal, was in charge. The boundary between the South Pacific Area and Southwest Pacific Area required cooperation between Halsey and MacArthur. Halsey's forces could penetrate into MacArthur's sphere with the permission of MacArthur. MacArthur, focused on retaking the Philippines, willingly worked with Halsey to defeat Rabaul.

For the Japanese, Rabaul was in their Southeast Area. The Southeast Area's western boundary was 140 east longitude, cutting through the middle of New Guinea. Its northern boundary was just above 1 degree north, on a line between Kapingamarangi and Nauru. From east of Nauru it ran southeast between the Fijis and Samoas, and then south. Rabaul was near the top of the region, roughly in its middle. This was a joint Imperial Japanese Army and Navy command. The land forces were commanded by General Hitoshi Imamura, while the Southeast Area's naval leader was Vice Admiral Jinichi Kusaka. In a rare example of inter-service harmony, the two leaders cooperated closely.

General Hitoshi Imamura commanded the Imperial Japanese Army forces within Japan's Southeast Area, headquartered at Rabaul. He remained after New Britain was cut off, as senior Japanese officer surrendering Rabaul at war's end. (USNHHC)

Planning begins

The Allies' first serious plan to take Rabaul was drafted in July 1942. The Joint Chiefs of Staff of the US Armed Forces sent a directive to the South and Southwest Pacific Area commanders to begin an advance against Rabaul. The directive was divided into three tasks. Task One directed the seizure of Guadalcanal, Tulagi, and the Santa Cruz Islands. Task Two called for recapturing the remaining Solomon Islands and northeastern coast of New Guinea. This included Japanese-held Lae, Salamaua, and points north. Task Three called for the occupation of New Britain, including Rabaul. Landings on Guadalcanal and Tulagi (occupation of the Santa Cruz Islands proved unnecessary), were scheduled for August 1942, but no deadlines were set.

In January 1943 the Casablanca Conference was held, defining Allied strategic objectives for the war. This meeting of the President of the United States, the Prime Minister of Great Britain, and the Combined Chiefs of Staff of both nations set the outline for the war. Defeating Germany and aiding the Soviet Union were given priority. A bomber offensive against Germany would start by mid-summer. China was to be kept in the war by recapturing Burma and reopening a supply road to China. The Allies were to maintain the offensive against the Japanese in the Southwest Pacific, including the recapture of Rabaul, but only resources unneeded elsewhere would be sent to the Southwest Pacific.

By February 1943, Task One goals had been achieved. MacArthur's staff drew up a plan, called *Elkton*, to complete Task Two and Task Three of the Joint Chiefs' objectives. It broke the tasks into five operations:

1. Seizing airfields on New Guinea's Huon Peninsula to provide bases for operations against Rabaul.
2. Seizing New Georgia and the new Japanese airfield on Munda Point to cover operations in the Northern Solomons.
3. Seizing airfields on Bougainville and New Britain outside the Gazelle Peninsula to support operations against Rabaul and Kavieng.
4. Capturing Kavieng to isolate Rabaul.
5. Capturing Rabaul.

This plan was discussed with Halsey. He agreed to support it. However, what had been learned at Guadalcanal and New Guinea was that removing Japanese land garrisons required commitments of large numbers of Allied troops and a significant expenditure of time and resources. When *Elkton* was reviewed in Washington the Joint Chiefs decided the resources needed to capture Rabaul were unavailable. Providing the required aircraft, especially heavy bombers, would cut into the bomber offensive against Germany. Several divisions of trained troops were available in the United States, but insufficient transports were available to move

Henderson Field, Guadalcanal in August 1942. Henderson Field served mainly as a base for heavy bombers during the aerial siege of Rabaul. (USNHHC)

the units to the Southwest Pacific and supply them once there. Few naval reinforcements could be provided, especially aircraft carriers. Prewar construction had been whittled down to two fleet carriers, and new construction was needed for a planned offensive in the Central Pacific. Any offensive against Rabaul would largely rely on assets already in the theater. Reinforcements would be limited to replacements for losses.

Elkton was re-written in late February, and a new plan presented to the Joint Chiefs in March. *Elkton II* was predicated on capturing airfields. The intention was to move airpower ever closer to Rabaul, isolating it before invading. Once Rabaul was ringed by airfields, so no reinforcements or supplies could reach it, ground troops could land, taking the city and harbor.

But even Rabaul isolated would be a tough nut to crack. Any Allied invasion force faced a force of nearly 100,000 men. This included an Imperial Japanese Army garrison of two infantry divisions, two infantry brigades, an artillery brigade, and an armor brigade. The Navy could contribute four naval guard units and a special naval landing unit, each equivalent to regimental strength.

In March 1943, including New Zealand, Australian, and US troops, the South and Southwest Pacific Areas had only the equivalent of 16 divisions available. Only six were combat ready. The rest were training or only suitable for garrison duty. Given commitments in New Guinea, and the troops required elsewhere in the theater, there were insufficient troops available to invade, much less take Rabaul.

However *Elkton II* suggested a solution, underscored by the results of the battle of the Bismarck Sea, where airpower alone stopped the Japanese reinforcing New Guinea. The solution was put forward in a further development, *Elkton III*: simply skip the invasion of Rabaul. Rabaul and its magnificent harbor were well-placed to support a Japanese invasion of Australia, but ill-positioned to support Allied operations to recapture the Philippines or take the Marianas. The Admiralties, north and west of Rabaul, offered a better location for a move to the Philippines and an adequate harbor, and would need to be taken in order to ring Rabaul.

Instead of Rabaul being occupied, it would be isolated and shorn of its airpower, and then could be largely ignored. Due to the mountainous terrain on New Britain, the Japanese garrison could not leave the Gazelle Peninsula, and the artillery and tanks there would have no influence beyond the range of their shells – perhaps 5 miles from the coast. A bypassed Rabaul would serve as an open-air internment camp for a major segment of the Japanese Pacific army, although Allied air raids would continue to weaken the garrison, guarantee air superiority, and prevent any rebuilding. Better still, as the Imperial Japanese were certainly not going to surrender, this internment camp would be self-run, and not draw on limited Allied logistics the way housing and feeding 100,000 prisoners of war would.

Preliminary conquests

The Huon Peninsula and New Georgia would still be taken, although Allied troops would still face off against entrenched Japanese ground forces. Control of the Huon Peninsula was needed not just as a springboard to Rabaul, but to secure Port Moresby and also the Vitiaz and Dampier Straits. These were needed for the march to the Philippines. The Japanese airbase at Munda on New Georgia threatened Guadalcanal and (if held by the Allies) permitted fighter cover as far north as Bougainville, another stepping stone to Rabaul.

Those were the only fortified positions to be taken, however. The rest of the plan called for seizing lightly defended islands circling New Britain and New Ireland where airfields could be built. A landing would be made, the island secured, and an airfield placed. Each island would be within fighter range of Allied air bases, allowing air cover while the airfield was under construction. Each new landing was closer to Rabaul, until single-engine Allied aircraft could reach that fortress. Landings would also be made on western and central New Britain, capturing Japanese airfields there. These were lightly garrisoned.

The most original part of the plan involved Bougainville. Geography and logistics dictated an Allied airfield on Bougainville. The Japanese had several airfields on the north and south ends of the island, as well as on Buka. These were heavily garrisoned. The Allied plan bypassed these. Instead, US Marines would land in the lightly held center of the island, establish a perimeter, and build airfields within that perimeter. The perimeter would be large enough to place the airfields outside the range of Japanese artillery, but no larger. Once established, Allied forces would entrench, and let the Japanese bleed trying to penetrate jungle fortifications.

The plan was risky because Bougainville was within easy range of Japanese fighters stationed around Rabaul and Japanese warships anchored at Simpson Harbor. The invasion fleet was gambling the US Navy could best the Imperial Japanese Navy's warships in surface night engagements, warfare at which the Japanese excelled. The odds against the Allies were increased because the heaviest available Allied surface units were light cruisers armed with 6in batteries, while the Japanese had several heavy cruisers packing both 8in batteries and Long Lance torpedoes. The rest of the Allied fleet, its fleet carriers, battleships, and heavy cruisers, were committed to the Central Pacific Area.

In order to reduce Rabaul, once other threats in the theater had been suppressed (most notably Japanese air assets in New

Dobodura was the first Allied airfield east of New Guinea's Owen Stanley mountain range. It shortened the flying distance to Rabaul and allowed aircraft to avoid a climb over the Owen Stanley Mountains while fully loaded. (USAAF)

OPPOSITE THE RABAUL THEATER: OCTOBER 1943–MAY 1944

Guinea and the Solomons) a concentrated air campaign would be turned against Rabaul. The five airfields around Rabaul and ships in Simpson Harbor and Blanche Bay were to be targeted first. Weather permitting, daily raids were to be conducted against the airfields and harbors. Runways were to be cratered, service buildings flattened, and aircraft destroyed. Ships would be sunk, wharves and loading facilities destroyed, and warehouses bombed. Accompanying Allied fighters would engage Japanese fighters.

Allied intelligence estimated the Japanese had 290 aircraft at Rabaul. The Japanese actually had 300 naval aircraft, reinforced by a monthly allotment of 50 aircraft. They could also call in another 200–300 from the Combined Fleet. Yet the Allies had a total of 1,800 aircraft in the area (including transports) and were building inventory. Given an ongoing campaign, Japan would eventually run out of fighters. Once this happened, Allied airpower would turn its attention to infrastructure, destroying warehouses, supply dumps and fuel depots, repair facilities, communications centers, barracks, and headquarters.

The ungainly PBY Catalina played an important offstage role during the siege of Rabaul. Black Cat Catalinas flew night missions against Japanese shipping and naval warships. Dumbo Catalinas rescued Allied flyers downed in the waters off New Britain and New Ireland. (AC)

The plan was delivered by General George Kenney, MacArthur's air commander. He had been fighting Rabaul since his arrival in July 1942. The Joint Chiefs approved, and the plan was implemented as Operation *Cartwheel*. It took time to grind through the initial stages – seizing the Woodlark Islands and Kiriwina, securing New Georgia, clearing the Huon Peninsula, and obtaining air superiority in New Guinea. By October 1943, these had been done.

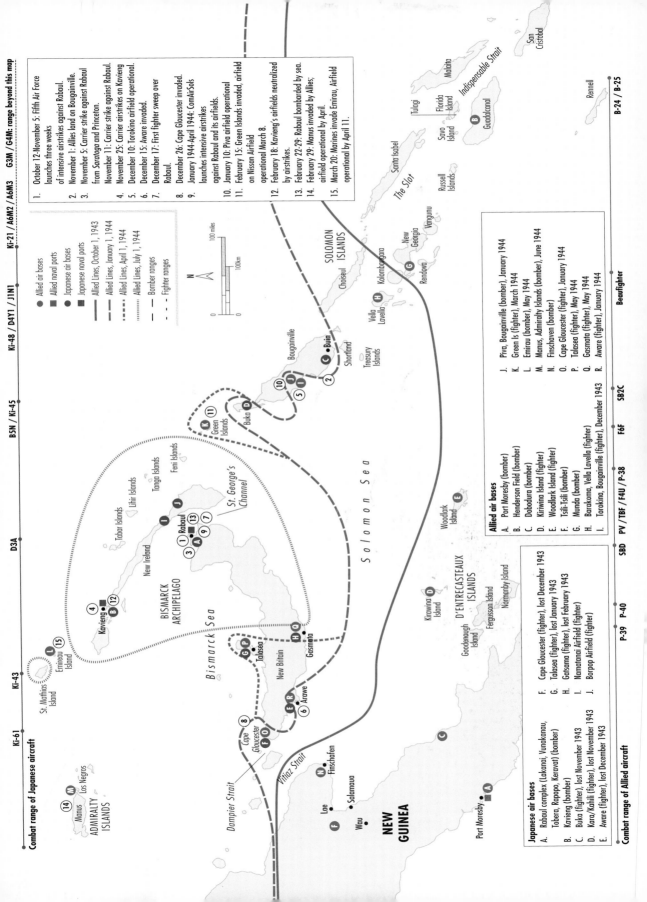

THE CAMPAIGN

Slowly tightening the noose

First air operations: 1942–43

An RAAF Beaufighter squadron participated in the first day's attack, strafing and bombing the Japanese airfield at Tobera. This picture shows an RAAF Beaufighter flying past New Guinea's Owen Stanley Mountains. (AC)

Although plans for the reduction of Rabaul were finalized in April 1943, it was six months before the air campaign against Rabaul started in earnest. In April only the Fifth Air Force, based in New Guinea, could reach Rabaul with fighter aircraft, its P-38s. The Fifth Air Force had mounted its first air attack against Rabaul in October 1942. It intermittently raided Rabaul and its airfields over the next eight months, but took these off its targeting list after June 1943. Too many other things took priority between mid-June and October. Late June and July were spent supporting the invasions of the Woodlarks and Kiriwina. August was consumed with reducing Wewak, Rabaul's aerial counterpart on New Guinea, and September saw the Fifth Air Force supporting the invasions of Lae and Finschhafen. Although necessary precursors to a Rabaul campaign, these operations forced the Fifth Air Force to neglect Rabaul.

The attention of Comairsols was consumed with operations in the Solomons. Spring saw invasions of the Russells. Summer was spent planning and executing the New Georgia invasion (culminating with the capture of the airfield at Munda). Fall saw planning and preparations for the invasion of Bougainville, scheduled for November 1. These activities absorbed all air resources in the Solomons, forcing Comairsols to ignore Rabaul.

As September ended, the Fifth Air Force completed priority activities in New Guinea and western New Britain. George Kenney was eager to revisit Rabaul. He viewed Wewak as a rehearsal for the big show at Rabaul. Taking Rabaul down a peg or two before the Bougainville landings would keep the Japanese off the backs of the invaders. Kenney also knew Bougainville airfields would bring Comairsols closer to Rabaul than the Fifth Air Force. If the Fifth Air Force were to knock out Rabaul before Bougainville's airfields came on line it had to act. Kenney believed one month's steady bombing would be enough.

Opening the siege: October 12–November 4, 1943

The Fifth Air Force returned to Rabaul in force on October 12. Kenney wanted to start earlier, but bad weather intervened. Photo-recon missions needed for pre-mission targeting kept getting scrubbed by clouds. Not until October 6 did recon aircraft, modified P-38 Lightnings, return with good photos. Additional flights were made on October 9, giving planners the latest information on ship and aircraft locations. The first mission indicated that Rabaul held only 184 aircraft: 87 twin-engine bombers, 37 single-engine bombers and 60 fighters. The later flight revealed the count had increased to 270. Aircraft to support Operation *RO* had arrived.

The totals did not affect Kenney's dispositions. He planned a maximum effort for his first strike. He sent everything he had: 115 B-25s, 87 B-24s, and 12 Bristol Beaufighters, escorted by 125 P-38s, a total of 339 aircraft. Including the weather and photo-recon aircraft sent out, over 350 Allied aircraft participated.

The B-25s left Dobodura at sunrise, and headed to Kiriwina, where they picked up a fighter escort, 78 P-38s. By the time the last of the B-25s had taken off, visibility at the airfield had dropped to zero due to dust. The Australian Beaufighters had to delay their departure until the dust settled. They finally became airborne at 0815hrs, but the late departure caused them to miss their fighter escort. The B-25s were assigned Vunakanau and Rapopo as targets. Five squadrons were to hit Vunakanau and three Rapopo. The Beaufighters were to strike Tobera.

While the B-25s were leaving Dobodura, B-24s from the 43rd and 90th Bombardment Groups were taking off from Port Moresby. With 6,000lb of bombs and a full load of gasoline, these aircraft were heavily laden. To allow for a fuel-conserving gradual climb to altitude, the heavies followed a path south around the tip of New Guinea, before heading east. As they crossed the Solomon Sea, they picked up an escort of 47 Lightnings from Kiriwina. Due to their longer flight path, they would arrive nearly two hours after the B-25s.

The medium bombers and their fighter escort flew over the Solomon Sea south of New Britain at virtually wave-top altitudes to stay under Japanese radar. They flew well south of Gasmata to avoid patrolling aircraft, turning north when they reached St George's Channel. They turned west at Wide Bay, using the mouth of the Warango River as a navigation point.

Even minutes from its targets, the Allied airstrike was still undetected. The Japanese had been lulled into complacency by the long Allied absence. Focused on preparations for Operation *RO* they had neglected the

The Fifth Air Force opened its offensive against Rabaul with attacks on three airfields. This photo shows B-25s attacking Vunakanau, using parachute bombs. Three G4M bombers in revetments are on the field. The picture was taken from an aft-pointing strike camera. (USAAF)

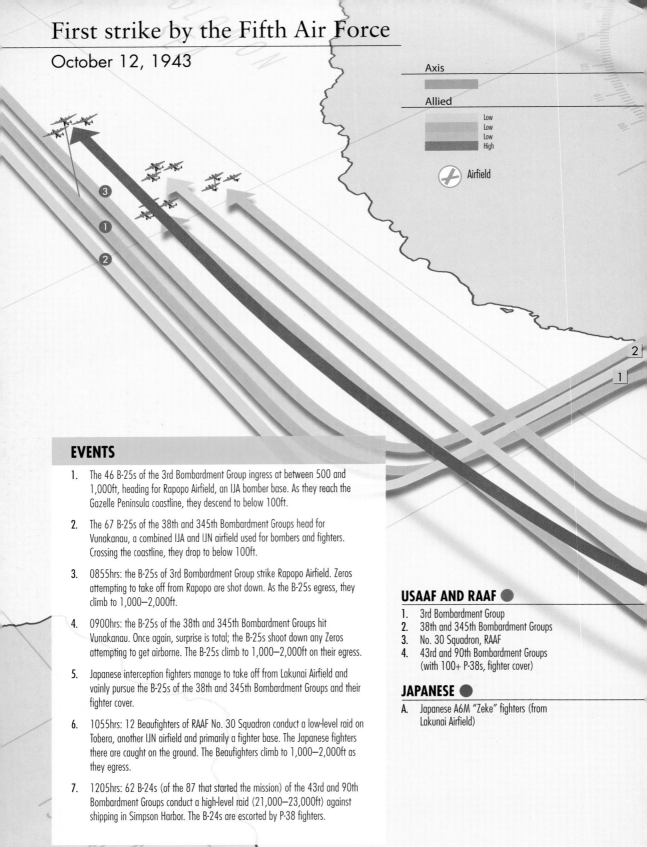

First strike by the Fifth Air Force
October 12, 1943

Axis

Allied

Low
Low
Low
High

✈ Airfield

EVENTS

1. The 46 B-25s of the 3rd Bombardment Group ingress at between 500 and 1,000ft, heading for Rapopo Airfield, an IJA bomber base. As they reach the Gazelle Peninsula coastline, they descend to below 100ft.

2. The 67 B-25s of the 38th and 345th Bombardment Groups head for Vunakanau, a combined IJA and IJN airfield used for bombers and fighters. Crossing the coastline, they drop to below 100ft.

3. 0855hrs: the B-25s of 3rd Bombardment Group strike Rapopo Airfield. Zeros attempting to take off from Rapopo are shot down. As the B-25s egress, they climb to 1,000–2,000ft.

4. 0900hrs: the B-25s of the 38th and 345th Bombardment Groups hit Vunakanau. Once again, surprise is total; the B-25s shoot down any Zeros attempting to get airborne. The B-25s climb to 1,000–2,000ft on their egress.

5. Japanese interception fighters manage to take off from Lakunai Airfield and vainly pursue the B-25s of the 38th and 345th Bombardment Groups and their fighter cover.

6. 1055hrs: 12 Beaufighters of RAAF No. 30 Squadron conduct a low-level raid on Tobera, another IJN airfield and primarily a fighter base. The Japanese fighters there are caught on the ground. The Beaufighters climb to 1,000–2,000ft as they egress.

7. 1205hrs: 62 B-24s (of the 87 that started the mission) of the 43rd and 90th Bombardment Groups conduct a high-level raid (21,000–23,000ft) against shipping in Simpson Harbor. The B-24s are escorted by P-38 fighters.

USAAF AND RAAF ⬤

1. 3rd Bombardment Group
2. 38th and 345th Bombardment Groups
3. No. 30 Squadron, RAAF
4. 43rd and 90th Bombardment Groups (with 100+ P-38s, fighter cover)

JAPANESE ⬤

A. Japanese A6M "Zeke" fighters (from Lakunai Airfield)

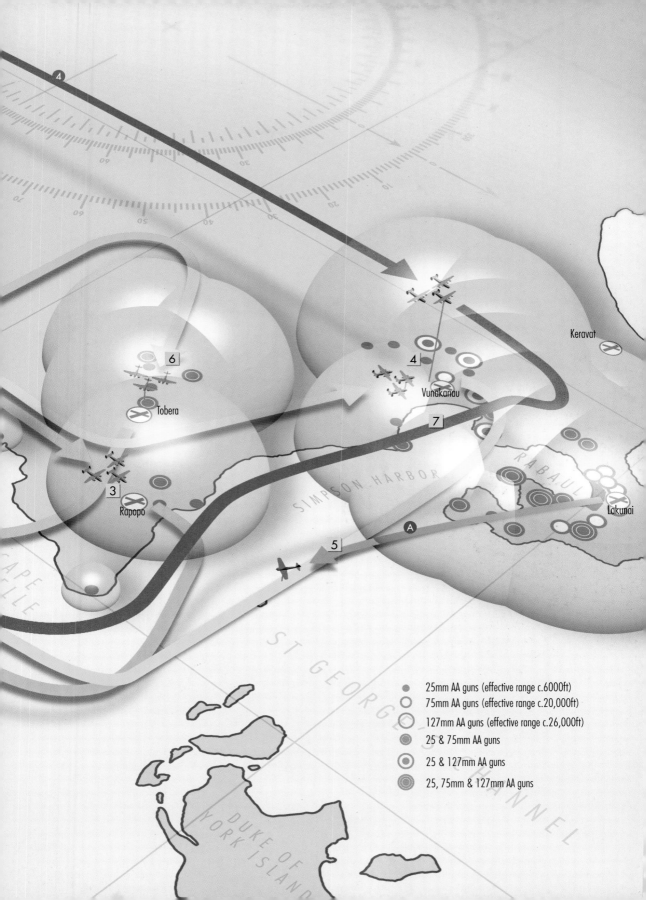

4

6

Tobera

3

Rapopo

4

Vunakanau

7

Keravat

RABAUL

Lakunai

SIMPSON HARBOR

A

5

CAPE
ELLE

ST GEORGE'S CHANNEL

DUKE OF
YORK ISLAND

- 25mm AA guns (effective range c.6000ft)
- 75mm AA guns (effective range c.20,000ft)
- 127mm AA guns (effective range c.26,000ft)
- 25 & 75mm AA guns
- 25 & 127mm AA guns
- 25, 75mm & 127mm AA guns

On November 2, 1943 the Fifth Air Force struck Simpson Harbor with 72 B-25s. One squadron armed with para-frag bombs strikes docks and harbor warehouses, damaging barges along the docks. (USAAF)

threat of an Allied attack. But they knew what a Fifth Air Force raid could do, for Kenney's boys had wiped out Wewak in August. The aircraft losses were so bad that in September most Imperial Army Air Force aircraft at Rabaul were transferred to Wewak as replacements.

Once over land, the B-25s split into two sections. The three squadrons of the 3rd Bomb Group turned north to Rapopo. The remaining five squadrons, from the 38th and 345th Bomb Groups, turned west to Vunakanau.

Rapopo, closer to Wide Bay, was hit first. Flying line-abreast at treetop level each squadron swept across Rapopo. Flying south to north, along the runway, the B-25s strafed the airfield with their eight .50-caliber nose guns. When over the airfield they dropped bundles of para-fragmentation bombs, 50–60 per aircraft. The parachutes slowed the descent long enough for the B-25s to clear the area before the bombs exploded. Three waves struck Rapopo, each squadron spaced 60–90 seconds apart. No sooner did the Japanese get up after one wave attacked than the next one came through.

Ten minutes later, the scene was repeated at Vunakanau. Instead of three waves, five waves hit Vunakanau. It was a larger airfield, so targets remained when the fifth squadron flew over, seven minutes after the first.

Surprise at both airfields was total. The first warning of trouble at Rapopo was the attacking Americans firing. Antiaircraft guns were covered with canvas when the first wave hit. Personnel were in the open, aircraft were on the ground. Even with ten minutes' warning, Vunakanau was little better prepared, with guns unmanned during the first strike. Although the guns were brought into action by the final waves, the gunfire was inaccurate and disorganized. Five Japanese fighters were in the air when the attack started, and were joined by others from Lakunai as the attack progressed, but only shot down one bomber.

Once they had finished their attacks, the B-25s headed to open water. The Rapopo strike force continued north until it reached St George's Channel, and followed that east and south around Cape Gazelle. The squadrons which had hit Vunakanau turned right, and flew south of Vulcan Crater and over Keravia Bay to reach St George's Channel.

Then, just before 1100hrs, the Beaufighters arrived. Tobera was smaller than the other two airfields, and inland. But the Japanese were alert, and the Australian aircraft were intercepted by 19 Zeroes over the airfield. The Beaufighters did less damage than the B-25s due both to their fewer numbers and to the smaller target.

Finally, at noon, the B-24s arrived. By now they were at altitude, 21,000–23,000ft high. They attacked the town of Rabaul and shipping in Simpson Harbor. By this time the Japanese were thoroughly alert and looking for trouble. Thirty-four fighters, probably launched from the untouched Lakunai fighter strip, met the Liberators. The escorting P-38s were largely ineffective, and several B-24s were damaged by attacking Japanese. Three failed to return to base, one ditching near Kiriwina.

The attack was a resounding success for the Fifth Air Force, although Kenney's claims were extravagant: over 150 aircraft destroyed on the ground, 26 Japanese fighters shot down, and three large transports, 43 small merchant ships, and 70 harbor craft sunk, with many more damaged. The actual results were less spectacular, but still impressive. Perhaps 60 aircraft were destroyed or badly damaged on the ground. Five fighters were shot down, including one shot down by a B-25 as it took off at Vunakanau. Ground personnel at Vunakanau and Rapopo took heavy casualties. Two fuel dumps were destroyed, and airfield buildings damaged. Seven warships had minor damage, and six cargo ships sunk, including an 8,500-ton naval auxiliary, two 550-ton sea trucks, and three smaller vessels. In exchange, the Allies lost five aircraft: three B-24s, one B-25, and one Beaufighter.

Kenney followed up the attack almost immediately. Twelve RAAF Beaufort torpedo bombers conducted a night raid against shipping in Simpson Harbor. Most failed to reach their target, with only two torpedoes launched and no hits. All 12 returned safely.

A larger follow-up was launched on October 13. Maintenance crews turned around virtually all aircraft overnight. In the morning, 70 B-24s left Port Moresby retracing the previous day's path, rendezvousing with 100 P-38s north of Kiriwina. Their target that day was Rabaul city, and its warehouses. The aircraft never reached their destination. The formation flew into a storm front halfway to New Britain. Visibility dropped to zero, and B-24s began icing. The mission was aborted and the planes returned home, the weather proving as deadly as the Japanese. One B-24 and three P-38s disappeared in the clouds. Weather prevented any further attacks on Rabaul for a week.

The storm fronts were south of New Britain, but the Japanese flew north of New Britain attacking New Guinea from Rabaul. The Japanese retaliated for the October 12 strike three days later. On October 15 a strike was sent against shipping in Oro Bay off New Guinea to cut supplies to Dobodura. This maximum Japanese effort consisted of 15 Aichi D3A (Val) dive bombers and 39 Zero fighters. Intercepted by P-38s and P-40s, the Japanese aircraft were shredded. Only one D3A returned to Rabaul and five Zeroes were shot down. Damage to shipping was trivial.

A follow-up attack two days later proved equally unrewarding. The Japanese sent 56 Zeroes on a fighter sweep to Dobodura. A slightly smaller number of US fighters met it. Eight Zeroes were splashed. The United States lost four P-38s and one P-40. It was the last time Japanese aircraft from Rabaul struck at Allied bases in New Guinea. The initiative was passing to the United States and its Anzac partners.

Since weather prevented it from raiding Rabaul following its October 13 strike, the Fifth Air Force instead visited Wewak. On October 18, good weather was expected and another major strike was launched. Kenney sent 77 B-24s, 54 B-25s, and nearly 100 P-38s to hit the airfields. The heavies were after Lakunai and Vunakanau, with the B-25s to strafe Rapopo and Tobera. The mission hit a stationary front south of New Britain. The Liberators and Lightnings turned back, but the leader of the Mitchells pressed on, despite the abort call.

Other B-25s hit ships in the harbor with 1,000lb bombs. A bomb falls aft of a transport during the attack on Simpson Harbor. Note the ship listing directly behind the attacked freighter. (USNHHC)

Three B-25 squadrons hit Rapopo, one hit Tobera, while one strafed shipping in Blanche Bay. But after hitting their targets, the unescorted bombers were jumped by 40 Japanese fighters. Two ships were damaged, and 11 Japanese fighters destroyed at the cost of three B-25s lost and six badly damaged.

The weather finally cleared on October 23, and daily raids began. October 23 saw 57 B-24s and 100 P-38s sent to bomb Lakunai and Vunakanau. These were clouded over; the bombers hit Rapopo instead. On October 24, 64 B-25s escorted by 54 P-38s strafed Vunakanau, Rapopo, and Tobera. Sixty-one B-24s with 50 escorting P-38s conducted high-level bombing of Vunakanau and Lakunai on October 25. On all three days, swarms of Japanese fighters – at least 40 Zeroes each day – met each raid. Earlier Japanese losses were replaced from reinforcements sent to support Operation *RO*. Fifth Air Force losses for all three days totaled one B-24, two B-25s, and two P-38s. The Japanese had 15 fighters shot down and six badly damaged in air-to-air combat, with over 60 aircraft destroyed or damaged on the ground. The Fifth Air Force believed it had done much better. Kenney claimed 86 aircraft destroyed on the ground and 100 shot down.

Then the weather closed things down again. A front stalled south of New Britain, providing a storm wall blocking raids from New Guinea, and giving the Japanese at Rabaul a four-day rest from the Fifth Air Force. They needed it. Their reconnaissance revealed that the United States was on the move in the Solomons. Halsey was preparing to invade Bougainville, and convoys were forming. The Japanese had been forced out of all their Solomon Islands airfields. The only opposition to this new Allied thrust had to come from Rabaul.

Admiral Kusaka called to Truk for help. By this time he had only ten dive bombers and 36 twin-engine *rikko* operational, too few to oppose the invasion. The Combined Fleet responded by sending everything available: the air groups of three veteran aircraft carriers; 150 aircraft from *Shokaku*, *Zuikaku*, and *Zuiho*. They arrived on November 1.

On October 29, the weather broke, letting Kenney resume his attacks against Rabaul. That day he sent one raid: 37 B-24s escorted by 53 P-38s. They conducted a high-altitude attack against Vunakanau. The Japanese scrambled 75 Zeroes to intercept them. The Japanese lost seven aircraft on the ground and six in the air. No US aircraft were shot down, but many were damaged. Although the Japanese were losing more aircraft and had fewer to start with, the cumulative damage was telling on both sides. Whereas the United States could send 100 fighters on October 12, they had only 53 operational on October 29.

Weather closed down the Fifth Air Force from October 31 through November 1. Kenney next raided Rabaul on November 2. This time he decided to go after the shipping in Simpson Harbor. The invasion of Bougainville had started on November 1, and Kenney believed Simpson Harbor would offer a target-rich environment. This time the Fifth Air Force dispatched nine B-25 squadrons and six P-38 squadrons – 75 B-25s and 57 P-38s, about half the strength mustered three weeks earlier.

Target-rich Simpson Harbor proved to be. In addition to the normal merchant traffic there, the Japanese had sent naval reinforcements from Truk: two heavy cruisers, two light cruisers, and two destroyers to augment the naval force stationed at Rabaul. These reinforcements were a little battered. They had fought a night engagement off Empress Augusta Bay during the pre-dawn hours of November 2. Their antiaircraft batteries were intact, however, adding to the already formidable array of guns ringing Simpson Harbor. Worse still, the Combined Fleet aerial reinforcements had arrived. The Fifth Air Force strike force was outnumbered. The attack was planned based on photo reconnaissance done following the November 29 raid. Planning missed both sets of reinforcements.

The Americans flew up the St George's Channel until they reached Crater Peninsula. They flew over the saddle formed by Mount Tovanurdatir and Mount Komvur. The raid started with two squadrons of P-38s strafing Lakunai. The Lightnings found their hands full. The Japanese had 100 fighters in the air, most from Lakunai. Having returned from a strike against the Bougainville invasion fleet that they had flown earlier in the day, some newly refueled Zeroes were taking off when the P-38s arrived.

Meanwhile the B-25s and the three squadrons of fighters escorting them flew over Rabaul and into Simpson Harbor. The B-25s attacked in squadrons, each squadron trailing the one ahead by one minute. The bombers were armed with a mix of para-fragmentation bombs, 1,000lb demolition bombs, and 100lb phosphorus bombs. While relatively unmolested by enemy aircraft (Japanese fighters initially concentrated on the Lightnings strafing Lakunai), the harbor attack force flew into a heavy concentration of antiaircraft artillery, both ashore and aboard the Japanese warships. To make the odds stiffer, the Japanese cruisers opened up with their main batteries against the low-flying strafers.

Back to base with the enemy in pursuit

On October 18, the Fifth Air Force launched a follow-up strike on Rabaul's airfields. It was intended as another maximum effort, but due to weather, a mission abort was declared. The B-24s and P-38s returned home, but 50 B-25s, led by Lieutenant Colonel Clinton True, pressed on, attacking Tobera and Rapopo airfields. A low-level raid on Tobera was successfully executed with the attacking squadron successfully escaping and evading all but a handful of pursuing fighters, but the Rapopo attack was not nearly as lucky. The three squadrons pasted the airfield with .50-caliber fire and daisy-cutters, but as soon as they cleared the coast they ran into a buzz-saw of Japanese fighters.

Having received warning of the impending raid, the two untouched airfields had sortied 40 Japanese fighters. They had been circling over the St George's Channel, expecting the P-38s which normally accompanied the bombers. Instead they discovered the trailing squadron of withdrawing Mitchells as they cleared the coast north of Rapopo. The Zeroes, a mixture of A6M2s and A6M3s, pounced on the unescorted bombers. A long battle followed as the Mitchells flew east, trying to clear Cape Gazelle.

The Zeroes ripped into the Mitchells, both singly and in pairs. For nearly 30 minutes the B-25s were pursued. The Zeroes flew in and out of the formation. The bombers tightened their formation, flying as close to each other as possible for mutual defense. They dropped down almost to wave-top heights to discourage diving attacks. The Japanese were so intent on their prey that some tried diving attacks anyway, misjudged the altitude, and struck the water. They continued their pursuit as the B-25s reached Cape Gazelle and turned south. Finally, the fighters thinned out, leaving the damaged bombers to complete the long trip home or divert to the closer Kiriwina.

MARK POSTLETHWAITE 2017

Post-strike reconnaissance photography captured the damage done. Docks are burning in the background. Several ships are damaged, and the ship in the foreground (numbered "7" in the intelligence photo) has been beached or is sinking. (USAAF)

The bombers gave as good as they got, strafing as they went in, and dropping their bombs. The battle over the harbor lasted nine minutes, with the flak defenses getting stiffer for each successive raid. The B-25s destroyed several floatplanes in the harbor, including a four-engine Kawinishi H8K ("Emily") flying boat. Four transports, including two 5,000-ton vessels, were sunk. Two heavy cruisers and one destroyer were damaged by near misses. Two dozen auxiliaries, from repair ships to tankers, were damaged. Eighteen Japanese aircraft were destroyed. In exchange, the Fifth Air Force lost nine B-25s and 12 P-38s. Nine of each were shot down, the rest destroyed in crash-landings at Dobodura or Kiriwina. Many others were damaged.

The Fifth Air Force flew only three more missions against Rabaul, on November 5, 7, and 10 in coordination with carrier airstrikes. These were relatively minor. Once the beachhead on Bougainville was secured, Kenney was content to turn over Rabaul to Comairsols. The Fifth Air Force turned its attention to New Guinea and western New Britain, particularly to support the invasions scheduled at Gatsama and Cape Gloucester. By Kenney's reckoning there was no further need for the Fifth Air Force: the Japanese had lost hundreds of aircraft and scores of ships. Nothing was left.

While the Japanese had suffered significant losses, they were still in the fight. It would take another four months to win air superiority over Rabaul. Comairsols had plenty to do.

The US Navy moves in: November 5–December 9, 1943

The neutralization of Rabaul was predicated on building Allied airfields on Bougainville. These permitted Allied fighters and single-engine bombers to reach Rabaul's airfields. They also saved wear on aircraft. The long-haul flights required by the Fifth Air Force were forcing more aircraft out of service due to maintenance issues than the Japanese destroyed in combat. Additionally, whereas flights from New Guinea were often stymied by stationary fronts in the Solomon Sea, these weather patterns were typically well west of the Solomon Islands. Weather offered fewer issues to Bougainville-based aircraft.

The Japanese expected an Allied landing on Bougainville, fortifying the airfields they had there. The United States bypassed these, landing in the lightly held middle of the island, off Empress Augusta Bay. They planned to seize and hold a perimeter just large enough to contain airfields safe from attack by Japanese artillery. The landing was made on November 1, successfully capturing the desired territory before the Japanese Army could counterattack.

Japanese aircraft proved unequal to disrupting the invasion fleet. Several attacks were launched from Rabaul, all involving fewer than 20 bombers. In each the sole result was the loss of most of the bombers sent and only minor damage inflicted on shipping in Empress Augusta Bay. Yet if Rabaul lacked the aircraft to repel the invaders, it did provide a base for warships to threaten that fleet. Allied air power made a daylight surface action suicidal, but Rabaul was only 200 nautical miles from Empress Augusta Bay. Fast warships could leave Rabaul in late afternoon, steam to Empress Augusta Bay, spend up to two hours in surface combat, and be back at Rabaul shortly after sunrise. The Japanese were masters of naval night combat.

Allied vulnerability in surface combat was aggravated by a lack of naval surface strength. The planned invasion of the Gilbert Islands in late November meant most of Halsey's cruisers and all of his battleships were in the Central Pacific. The only surface forces Halsey could call on were four Cleveland-class light cruisers. But these, in concert with eight Fletcher-class destroyers sufficed to defeat the Japanese – two heavy cruisers, two light cruisers, and six destroyers – at the battle of Empress Augusta Bay on November 2.

Admiral Koga, commanding the Combined Fleet at Truk, decided to reinforce Rabaul. For over a year he had husbanded his cruisers for the right moment. He decided that time had been reached. He sent seven heavy cruisers: *Takao*, *Maya*, *Atago*, *Suzuya*, *Mogami*, *Chikuma*, and *Chokai*, along with the light cruiser *Noshiro* and four destroyers as an escort, and a fleet train of two tankers. When combined with the *Myoko* and *Haguro*, already at Rabaul, these created a task force large enough to overwhelm the American cruiser screen with plenty left over to destroy any transports or cargo ships off Bougainville.

American reconnaissance discovered the arriving ships on November 4, heading towards St George's Channel. It was too late to get surface reinforcements to Empress Augusta

The morning of November 5, 1943 found USS *Saratoga* and *Princeton* off Bougainville preparing to attack Rabaul. Preparations are made on *Saratoga's* flight deck to launch aircraft for the strike. (USNHHC)

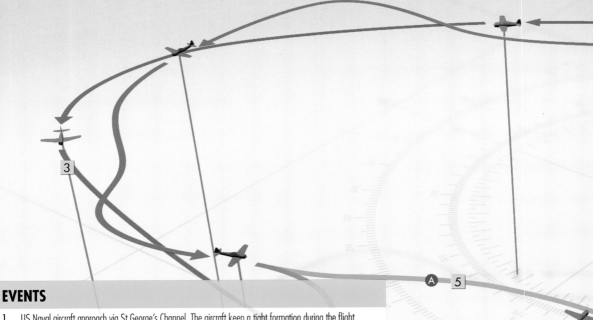

EVENTS

1. US Naval aircraft approach via St George's Channel. The aircraft keep a tight formation during the flight. At the bottom (c.12,000ft) are the TBFs, accompanied by 17 F6Fs (one flying close escort for the command bomber). Approximately 1,000ft above that are the SBDs; 2,000ft above them are 16 F6Fs. Flying top cover another 2,000ft above these aircraft are 19 more F6Fs. There are 97 aircraft – 23 TBF Avenger torpedo bombers, 22 SBD Dauntless dive bombers, and 52 F6F Hellcat fighters – on the mission.

2. The Japanese have launched 70 aircraft in response – 65 various types of the A6M "Zero" fighters, and five D4Y1 Judy bombers, which are to fly over the American bombers and drop time-fused phosphorous bombs intended to explode among the US bombers (it did not work.) The Japanese are circling at c.16,000ft over Lakunai airfield, with another group approaching from the west, as the US aircraft get nearer. When the USN formation reaches Blanche Bay, they move to intercept, but wait outside the formation for it to break up, feeling it would be easy to shoot down the bombers once the formation has broken up.

3. The USN planes make a 180-degree turn at Tavui Point, and then drop down from 15,000ft to 10,000ft as they approach Simpson Harbor.

4. Japanese antiaircraft opens fire as the USN planes fly over Rabaul. The USN aircraft now break their tight formation for individual attack as they reach Simpson Harbor. The idea is to attack the Japanese warships along their length and from behind. The wind is from the southeast, meaning most anchored ships are pointing to the northwest.

5. Rather than risk their own AA fire, the Japanese aircraft fly around Simpson Harbor.

6. Cmdr Howard Caldwell in the command TBF begins directing attacks against Japanese shipping in the harbor. His command TBF plane, escorted by two F6Fs, circles at 10,000ft.

7. The SBD Dauntless dive bombers attack the warships in groups of two or three as directed by Clifton's command plane. They dive down at a 70–80 degree angle from 10,000ft, drop bombs between 2,000 and 1,000ft, and then level off to 500ft. They hit five out of six heavy cruisers, with a near-miss one of the light cruisers

8. The TBF Avenger torpedo bombers in teams of three spiral down to 250ft and make torpedo attacks on cruisers and moving ships (mainly destroyers). Only two torpedoes hit: both are duds.

9. The F6F Hellcat fighters engage and pursue the Japanese Zeros after the formation unpacks.

10. Four to six Japanese fighters engage Cmdr Howard Caldwell's TBF and his escorts. They dive south out of the mouth of Blanche Bay, chased by the Japanese fighters.

11. All USN aircraft race down St George's Channel after attacking, where they reform for the trip home, pursued by the Japanese fighters.

US Navy airstrike against Simpson Harbor

November 5, 1943

US NAVY UNITS ●

1. Combined flight paths of all attacking US Navy aircraft (before split)
2. TBF Avenger torpedo bomber (commander), escorted by two F6F Hellcats
3. TBF Avenger torpedo bombers (23)
4. SBD Dauntless dive bombers (22)
5. F6F Hellcat fighters (52)

JAPANESE ●

A. A6M "Zero" fighter, and five D4Y1 Judy bombers
B. A6M "Zeros"

Axis

Allied

Airfield

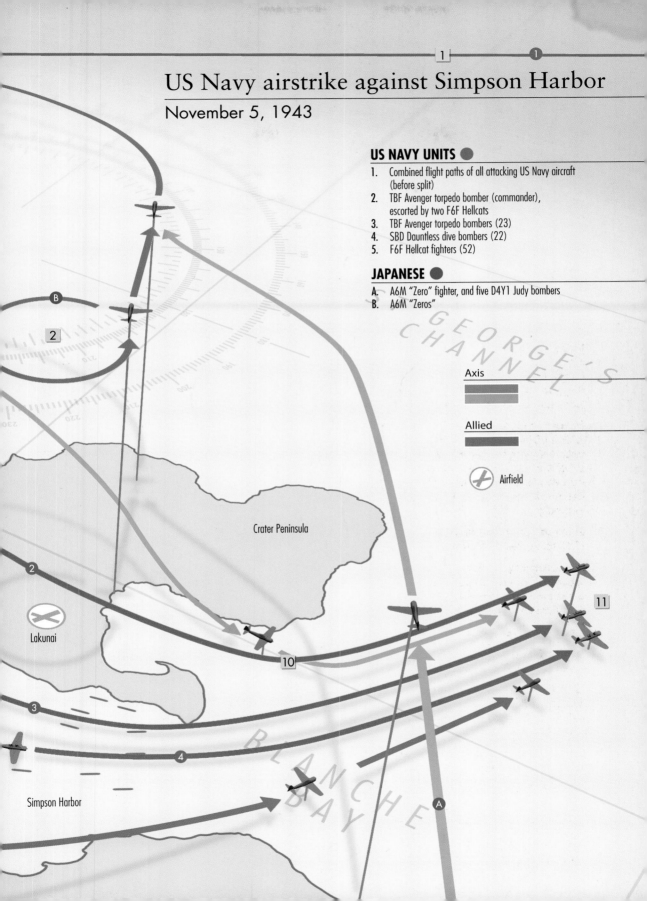

ST GEORGE'S CHANNEL

Crater Peninsula

Lakunai

Simpson Harbor

BLANCHE BAY

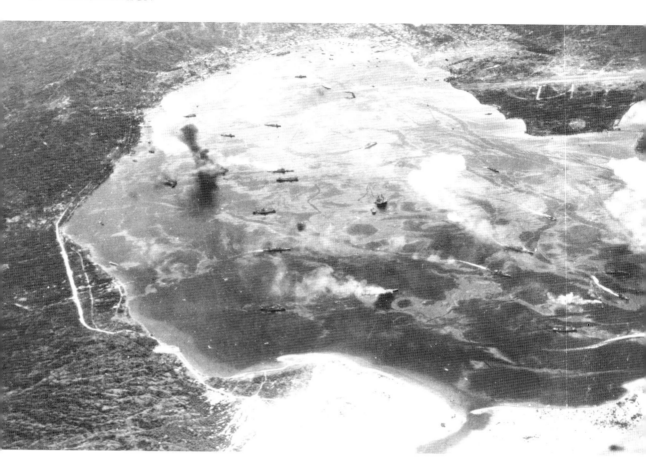

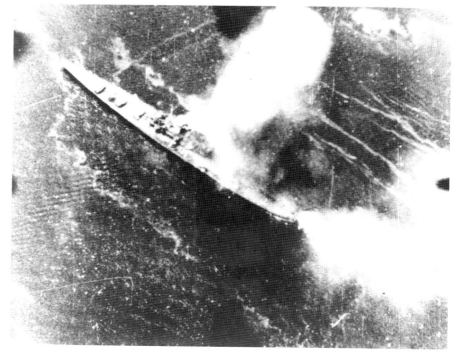

ABOVE Simpson Harbor near the beginning of the November 5 raid. Cruisers are anchored, bows pointing towards the prevailing wind. At least one cruiser has already been hit. This photograph was taken by the command TBF by Photographer's Mate First Class Paul T. Barnet. (USNHHC)

RIGHT A gun camera photo taken by a *Saratoga* SBD shows the heavy cruiser *Chikuma* damaged by a near miss from a bomb landing amidships near the starboard side. *Chikuma* was one of five heavy cruisers damaged by the US Navy's November 5 raid on Rabaul. (USNHHC)

Bay. Unless some way existed to eliminate the threat posed by these Japanese cruisers, the invasion was at risk.

Halsey had an aircraft carrier task force. It consisted of *Saratoga*, a fleet carrier, but the oldest carrier in the US Navy, the light carrier *Princeton*, two Atlanta-class antiaircraft cruisers and nine destroyers. Their aircraft had supported the invasion three days earlier. The task group was off Guadalcanal, refueling. Halsey staff quickly put together a plan to hit Rabaul with a carrier airstrike.

It was risky. Naval intelligence pegged Japanese strength at over 150 aircraft. The two carriers could send fewer than 100 and that only by including every fighter, leaving the task force with no air cover. The naval aircraft's short range meant the carriers had to move well north parallel to Bougainville and within range of Rabaul-based Japanese bombers. But it was the only way to take out the heavy cruisers. Kenney's strafer B-25s were ineffective against heavy cruisers as they demonstrated on November 2, against *Myoko* and *Haguro*.

Halsey ordered the strike. To get to the launch point by dawn, the task force, commanded by Admiral Frederick Sherman, steamed north at 30 knots. Cloud cover shielded the carriers from Japanese observation. One patrol plane spotted the ships, and told Rabaul that it consisted of cruisers and destroyers.

Halsey directed Sherman to send everything. The carriers would be protected by shore-based Navy and Marine Corsairs, flying out of Munda.

On November 5, 97 aircraft were launched: 52 F6F Hellcat fighters, 23 Avenger torpedo bombers, and 22 Dauntless dive bombers. The pilots planned the attack as they flew to Simpson Harbor. The prevailing wind was from the south-southeast. Ships anchored in Simpson Harbor would have their bows pointing toward the wind. Both torpedo and dive bombers are most effective if they approach the target ship in the direction of the fore–aft axis of the ship, as this maximizes their chances of hitting the target. Torpedo bombers flew parallel to the ship's length, and then turned towards the ship to launch torpedoes. Dive bombers dove on the ship along its length.

The mission commander decided to fly down the St George's Channel until they were north of Crater Peninsula, turn south over the peninsula, and attack Simpson Harbor from the north. This route also allowed the planes to escape out the mouth of the harbor. For once everything went right for the Americans. They arrived shortly after the Japanese fleet. It had anchored and was fueling in preparation for the attack planned that night.

Japanese radar gave warning of the raid, and the flight past Crater Peninsula gave the 70 Japanese fighters scrambled time to meet the American formation. They followed the formation but did not attack, waiting until the US formation split up. Instead the Navy aircraft held formation until they were over Simpson Harbor. There, every antiaircraft gun ashore and afloat opened up, while the Japanese fighters remained outside the curtain of flak.

It was too late, and the flak was ineffective. Two Japanese cruisers were finishing fueling. One, *Maya*, took a hit in the aircraft deck. The bomb exploded in the engine room, killing 70 and wounding 60. *Atago* took three near misses, causing hull damage below the waterline. *Takao* and *Mogami* each took a single hit – in both cases between the two forward turrets, leaving 40 percent of their main batteries unusable. *Chikuma* was damaged by a near miss. Of the heavy cruisers, only *Suzuya* was undamaged. Light cruisers *Agano* and *Noshiro* were also hit, as were two destroyers, one by a dud torpedo.

The Japanese fighters pounced after the bombs were dropped and the US aircraft were streaking out of harbor. By then it was too late. The fighters soon peeled off to meet a new threat: 27 B-24s and 67 P-38s sent to attack Rabaul. They struck the docks at 1225hrs, an hour after the carrier planes attacked. They met only light fighter opposition, as the Navy's raid had drawn off most of the Japanese fighters.

American aircraft losses were light. The Navy lost nine aircraft, while one P-38 was shot down. In exchange, Hellcats shot down two Zeroes, one D4Y1 (which had been dropping

Navy personnel remove casualties from the air group commander's TBF, following a one-wheel landing with no flaps, ailerons, or radio on *Saratoga* after being shot up over Rabaul. Tail gunner Kenneth Bratton was wounded and photographer Paul Barnett killed by a fighter attacking the TBF. Commander Henry H. Caldwell, the pilot, climbs from his cockpit. (USNHHC)

phosphorus bombs on the US formation) and one twin-engine bomber unfortunate enough to be taking off from Tobera when an escaping Hellcat flew past it. At 1640hrs, after *Saratoga* and *Princeton* recovered their aircraft, the task force headed south as fast as they had steamed north.

Admiral Takeo Kurita, commanding the cruiser force, was furious. In response Kusaka sent scouts seeking the American carriers. They found the task force just before it headed south. Kusaka sent 14 B5N2 torpedo bombers after the carriers. The bombers reported sinking two aircraft carriers. In reality they came across a three-ship convoy consisting of PT-167 and two landing craft. The torpedoes, set for deep draft ships, all underran their targets, except for two that porpoised. One struck an LCI above the waterline and failed to explode. A second went through PT-167. Four B5N2s failed to return, including one shot down by the PT boat and a second which crashed after striking a mast.

Although the US airstrike failed to sink a single ship, it achieved its purpose. Five of the six heavy cruisers at Rabaul were damaged. Three required dockyard repairs. The midnight cruiser sortie was canceled; the Bougainville beachhead was reprieved. The Imperial Japanese Navy pulled its heavy warships out of Rabaul, and never returned.

The US Navy was not through with Rabaul. Because of the crisis in the Solomons Nimitz sent a second carrier task force to Halsey. It was a temporary loan, only until November 14, when it had to return to the Central Pacific to support the Gilbert Islands landings. Due to difficulties finding an adequate destroyer screen, the carriers remained in port until November 8. This resulting group consisted of the Essex-class carriers *Essex* and *Bunker Hill*, light carrier *Independence*, and nine destroyers. They carried 211 aircraft: 96 F6F Hellcats, 46 TBF Avengers, 36 SBD Dauntlesses, and 33 SB2C Helldivers, the combat debut of the new dive bomber.

Halsey decided to make a second carrier strike against Rabaul. This one, launched November 11, involved both carrier groups and over 300 aircraft. Sherman's task force with *Saratoga* and *Princeton* struck from the east, launching from a spot near the Green Islands 225 nautical miles from Rabaul. The new task force, commanded by Rear Admiral Alfred Montgomery, launched from southeast of Rabaul. Its aircraft left the flight deck when the carriers were 160 nautical miles from Rabaul, a lot closer than Sherman.

Since the attack occurred a week after the November 5 strike, most of the heavy cruisers were already gone, back to either Truk or the Home Islands for repairs. Only *Maya* was still there, receiving repairs to its engine to allow it to reach Japan. There were still several light cruisers and numerous destroyers and auxiliary vessels in Simpson Harbor, though. While the pickings were fewer, they were still significant. There were also fewer aircraft for the Allies to face. The Japanese were down to 270 aircraft. The Rabaul-based contingent had lost 44 aircraft in a week, while the carrier aircraft were down 39. Truk was scheduled to send 28 more aircraft, but they did not arrive before the American carrier aircraft visited.

Halsey again requested assistance from the Fifth Air Force. Kenney sent 20 Beaufort torpedo bombers on a nighttime strike at Simpson Harbor on November 9–10, which accomplished little. A B-24 raid on November 11 was washed out by weather.

Weather affected the Navy as well. Sherman's group attacked first, but Rabaul was socked in. The aircraft from *Saratoga* and *Princeton* played hide-and-seek with Japanese warships ducking in and out of rain squalls. They attacked a light cruiser and four destroyers on their first strike, inflicting only minor damage. Weather washed out a second strike, but it was able to withdraw undetected.

Montgomery's strike went better. Skies were clearer when they went in. Torpedo bombers managed to score hits on the light cruiser *Agano* and destroyer *Naganami*. A Helldiver planted a bomb on the destroyer *Suzunami*. It was loading torpedoes when hit and the bomb and sympathetic detonations shattered the hull. Three other destroyers and a light cruiser received minor damage from the bombers.

The Japanese scrambled 107 fighters to meet the carrier planes. A combination of flak and Japanese fighters would bring down nine US aircraft: four Avengers and five Hellcats. Four Hellcats, two Helldivers, and one Avenger reached the carriers, but were so badly

Commander Joseph C. Clifton, USN, who commanded VF-12, *Saratoga*'s fighter squadron, passes out cigars in the wardroom afterwards, celebrating the successful November 5 air attack on Rabaul. (USNHHC)

RIGHT The Japanese sought the US carriers following the November 5 attack. Instead of finding the carriers, they found and attacked two landing craft and PT-167. A B5N-launched aerial torpedo struck PT-167 but passed through the boat without exploding. (USNHHC)

BELOW US carriers made a second Rabaul air strike on Veterans' Day. The Japanese found and attacked one American carrier task force. Here a Japanese torpedo bomber explodes astern of USS *Essex* after being shot down by antiaircraft fire. All 14 B5Ns sent were shot down. (USNHHC)

damaged they ditched next to the carriers. Thirty other planes returned with battle damage. In exchange, 11 Japanese fighters were shot down.

To permit the largest possible airstrike against Rabaul, 24 Corsairs from VF-17, a land-based Navy squadron in the Solomons, reattached their tail hooks and flew top cover over Montgomery's task force while the strike was launched. Once the strike was away, they landed on the carriers and refueled. By noon, as the Rabaul strike was returning, they were aloft again. It was as well, because Kusaka's scouts found Montgomery's ships. At noon Kusaka sent well over 100 aircraft in pursuit. American radar detected the force at 1313hrs, 120 miles away.

Montgomery was preparing a second strike against Rabaul. To clear the flight deck he launched these aircraft ten minutes later. Twenty minutes after that, American fighters intercepted the Japanese aircraft, 40 miles from the carriers. A massive dogfight ensued, with some of the bombers launched for the canceled second strike joining US fighters in attacking. Over the next 30 minutes the sky rained bombs, torpedoes, and shot-down aircraft. Although the Japanese launched eight torpedoes at the carriers, all missed. None of the dive bombers put a bomb on a target either.

The Japanese lost most of their bombers. All 14 B5N torpedo bombers were shot down by US fighters or flak, as were 17 of the 25 D3A dive bombers, four D4Y1 bombers, and perhaps three G4M *rikko*. Only two Zeroes failed to return, but one of the planes was flown by the commander of *Zuiho*'s fighter squadron, Lieutenant Masao Sato, a Pearl Harbor veteran. In exchange the US Navy lost six aircraft. Two Corsairs ditched when they ran out of fuel, two Hellcats were shot down, a patrolling Helldiver disappeared (presumably shot down by the outbound Japanese), and one Avenger was destroyed in an accident.

Extravagant claims were made by both sides. The Japanese claimed to have sunk a cruiser and damaged two aircraft carriers. US Navy flyers claimed 86 aircraft shot down. The best assessment of the exchange was made by Admiral Koga. He ordered all cruisers out of Rabaul, and never again used it as a base for his surface ships. Additionally, on November 12, Koga withdrew the surviving carrier aircraft sent to Rabaul two weeks earlier. Of the 150 aircraft sent, just over 100 remained. Rabaul's permanent air garrison had lost a similar percentage of aircraft. As replacements, Koga withdrew aircraft stationed in the Marshalls, transferring them to Rabaul. The transfer worked to the benefit of the United States, which invaded the Marshalls in January 1944.

After November 12 the US Navy dominated the waters around the northern Solomons. Less than two weeks later a flotilla of US destroyers intercepted a Japanese run to Bougainville. The battle fought just south of Cape St George on New Ireland saw three Japanese destroyers sunk with no damage to the American ships. Rabaul effectively ceased to be a naval base.

Fighter siege: December 10–January 6, 1944

October and November heralded a turning point: Rabaul's garrison shifted to a strictly defensive posture after mid-November. They lacked the aircraft to effectively attack Allied bases in the Solomons or New Guinea. They launched a series of airstrikes against the Bougainville beachhead on November 17 but the results were dismal. In exchange for sinking one fast transport (a converted World War I-era destroyer), the Japanese lost 14 aircraft. The loss rate was unsustainable, even if the inflated claims of five ships sunk had been true. The withdrawal of the cruisers to safer waters left the Allied ships off Bougainville unthreatened by surface warships – and even meant the Japanese were unable to meet the US Navy in the waters around Rabaul.

For the next few weeks, from November 12 through December 16, the daytime skies over the Gazelle Peninsula remained quiet. Except for nighttime intruder raids against Simpson Harbor and Rabaul by Australian Beauforts, the Allies remained out of the skies over Eastern New Britain. This was as well for Kusaka and his aviators. By mid-November, the Allied assault had whittled down Rabaul's air garrison to 110 operational aircraft. Its paper strength exceeded 200 aircraft, but many had combat damage or were unflyable due to wear. The pause gave them a brief opportunity to recuperate.

Yet the pause was a reprieve and not a pardon. The carriers had left to support operations in the Central Pacific. Comairsols was focusing its attention on supporting the beachhead at Empress Augusta Bay. The Fifth Air Force was absorbed by supporting preparations for landings in western New Britain.

On Bougainville, US Marines gouged out a toehold in the center of Bougainville large enough for airfields. By Christmas Day the perimeter was 6¼ miles wide and 4½ miles deep. Navy Seabees and New Zealand combat engineers started work on an airstrip just off the beach next to Cape Torokina literally days after the November 1 landing. On November 24 it received its first arrival, a flak-damaged Marine SBD.

The Torokina airfield was crude, but effective. In three weeks Seabees had graded a single 4,750ft by 200ft strip of beach, covered it with a layer of coral, and topped it with metal planking. It still lacked taxiways, hardstands, and buildings on that date, but these were soon added. On December 10, the airfield was declared operational.

Nor was Torokina the only airfield built on Bougainville. As the Marines pushed inland the Seabees and engineers followed. They began carving two additional landing strips in jungle 3 miles inland. One was a mile long. The second, intended for bombers, was 8,000ft long. Work started on the bomber strip on November 29 and on the fighter strip on December 10. Unlike the Japanese airfields on the Gazelle Peninsula, which took upwards of a year to complete, both were finished within a month. The bomber strip was operational on December 30, with the fighter strip completed by January 3. As with Torokina, these two airstrips, Piva Uncle and Piva Yoke, were covered by coral and surfaced with metal planking.

Bougainville was not the only place where new Allied airfields were emerging. On December 16, 1943 Allied forces landed on Arawe, a small island just off the southwest corner of New Britain. The objective was a shallow-draft harbor to base motor torpedo boats. Then, on December 26, the US First Marine Division landed at Cape Gloucester, on the northwest end of New Britain. Both sites had existing airfields built by the Japanese back when New Britain was intended as the springboard to Australia. By December 1943 both were largely abandoned, with no permanent air garrison and lightly held by land forces. The Japanese could only reinforce these sites by sea, as the road network joining the two ends of the island was notional rather than real. Since the Fifth Air Force and Comairsols controlled the waters around New Britain the garrisons were on their own.

The Allies soon improved both airfields, paving both with steel planking. Neither airfield proved particularly useful, however. The Bougainville fields were closer to Rabaul and New Ireland. Arawe and Cape Gloucester were ill-placed for supporting further Allied advances – except perhaps towards the Gazelle Peninsula and Rabaul, an idea long since abandoned. It was, however, a further signal that the Rising Sun was setting.

Torokina's opening marked the beginning of the end for Rabaul. The day after it was declared operational eight Corsairs from the Marine VMF-214 squadron landed at Torokina to refuel. The squadron's commander, Greg "Pappy" Boyington, had landed there the previous day and found it adequate. The other pilots of his renowned "Black Sheep" squadron agreed.

Corsairs fueled at Torokina could reach Rabaul and return with reasonable fuel reserves. Boyington's squadron, along with other Marine and Navy fighter squadrons, had been stationed at Munda on New Georgia. Although these squadrons would soon be transferred to Torokina Boyington realized they could strike Rabaul even before the transfer. He proposed a fighter sweep with aircraft based at Munda landing at Torokina, refueling, and then going to Rabaul.

LEFT The Curtiss SB2C-1 "Helldiver" scout bomber made its appearance over Rabaul on the November 11 air strike flying off USS *Bunker Hill*. Helldivers were also used in raids on Kavieng, on New Ireland. (USNHHC)

BELOW Seabees carry sections of pressed steel runway surfacing, building the Torokina airfield in December 1943. This base allowed single-engine fighters like the Corsair, Hellcat, and Kittyhawk to reach Rabaul. (USNHHC)

Major Gregory Boyington, USMCR commanding Marine Fighter Squadron VMF-214, waves while taxiing his F4U Corsair at Torokina. Boyington led the first fighter sweep against Rabaul on December 17, 1943. He was shot down and captured on January 3, 1944. (USNHHC)

Everyone wanted to get into the act and participate in the first sweep. VMF-214 found itself joined by the rest of the Marine Corsairs, Navy F6Fs, and RNZAF Kittyhawks (an export version of the P-40E). The sweep did not take place until December 17. That day 32 Corsairs, 24 F6Fs, and 24 Kittyhawks took off from airfields at New Georgia and Vella Lavella, rendezvoused at Torokina, topped off their fuel tanks, and headed to Rabaul.

The three types of aircraft had different flying characteristics and different cruising speeds. The Kittyhawks, slowest of all, took off first. The plan was for them to come in at 15,000ft, and draw in the Japanese. Next came the Hellcats, flying above the Kittyhawks. The last to leave were the Corsairs, who flew top cover. It was a long flight over open water, calculated to make the pilot of a single-engine aircraft nervous. If the engine failed it was a long swim home.

The battle started as planned, with the Kittyhawks getting the jump on the Zero fighters scrambled to meet them. The Japanese had reinforced Rabaul in response to the Arawe landings, and were able to launch 35 fighters to meet the Allied fighters. After the Kittyhawks made their first pass, shooting down a Japanese fighter, the advantage switched to the more agile Japanese. The squadron leader's P-40 was fatally damaged and a second Kittyhawk went down after colliding with a Zero. Remarkably, both pilots survived.

Meanwhile both the F6Fs and Corsairs, at high altitudes, were coming up empty. The Corsairs circled Lakunai field without finding targets. Boyington exchanged insults with an English-speaking Japanese officer over the radio, but despite his challenges found no targets in the air. When all aircraft returned to base, the score was even. Two Kittyhawks and two Zeroes were lost; one each due to the collision and one shot down by both sides.

Post-mission evaluations concluded that too many aircraft had been sent on that first sweep. Control proved impossible on that scale. Future sweeps were scaled down, but the December 17 mission set a pattern which would be followed for the next three weeks. Fighters flying out of Torokina, often staged from airfields further south, would grind down Rabaul's air garrison.

It was an attrition battle, one favoring the Allies. In mid-December the Japanese had 140 fighters and 110 bombers available for the defense of Rabaul. That number included aircraft normally stationed at Gasmata in central New Britain and on New Ireland which could assist the 100 fighters and 75 bombers flying out of Gazelle Peninsula fields. The Allies within Comairsols had 200 fighters, 200 light and medium bombers, and 100 heavy bombers operational – with 70 fighters and 60 bombers in reserve, undergoing maintenance and repair.

Even when the 50-odd operational P-39s were excluded from the Allied fighter tally, the Japanese barely managed parity with the Allies. And, except for those P-39s, the Allied fighters were equal to or superior to the Japanese *Reisen*, especially the 130 or so Hellcats and Corsairs. A further handicap for the Japanese was logistics and personnel. The Allies could replace destroyed aircraft and injured aircrew. The Japanese could not. Their aircraft replacement rate was below their loss rate, they had few aircrew replacements, and many of the pilots at Rabaul were grounded. Nearly one-third were suffering from malaria or other tropical diseases.

The next Comairsols raid on Rabaul took place December 19. A follow-up raid had been planned for December 18, but was washed out due to summer rains common in a Southern Hemisphere December. Weather affected the December 19 attack. Of 48 B-24s sent, 32 turned back. The 16 remaining bombers were escorted by 51 Allied fighters: P-38s, Kittyhawks, and Corsairs. The Japanese sortied 94 fighters in response, but were as affected by the weather as the Allies. Less than half made contact with the enemy. In the resulting melees, five Zeroes were shot down. Ten Allied aircraft were lost, but only two shot down. The other eight were due to a mid-air collision and landing mishaps, all near home.

Storm fronts prevented an Allied return to Rabaul until December 23. On that mission, B-24s escorted by Corsairs and Hellcats bombed Lakunai. Radar gave the Japanese early warning and nearly 100 Zeroes were scrambled. Sixty made contact with the bombers. The bombers were jumped by the fighters after successfully hitting Lakunai. No bombers were lost, but two Corsairs were shot down in the ensuing dogfights. The twist was that the Americans followed up the raid with a fighter sweep: 48 Corsairs. They arrived 15 minutes after the bombers left, surprising the airborne Japanese fighters, most of which lacked radios. Six *Reisen* were shot down, several others damaged. It was a good exchange for two Corsairs.

The Allies returned on the following two days. On December 24, the fighter sweep preceded the bombers. The Allies claimed 18 kills, but probably downed only six, while the Japanese claimed 55 (a total greater than the fighters sent), but shot down six RNZAF Kittyhawks and one Hellcat. A bombing raid on Christmas Day saw each side lose three fighters.

On that same day, the Navy launched a carrier raid against Kavieng, while the Army landed on Cape Gloucester. The raid on Kavieng was conducted by a carrier task group consisting of the Essex-class USS *Bunker Hill* and the Independence-class *Monterey*. It served a dual purpose: to distract attention from the landings at Cape Gloucester and to interdict sea traffic between Truk and Rabaul. The attack sank a 5,000-ton freighter and a minesweeper, as well as damaging several other ships. The task group conducted several more raids against Kavieng through January 4, shooting down ten Japanese fighters during these raids and further isolating Rabaul.

Comairsols took Boxing Day off, but conducted fighter sweeps over Rabaul on December 27 and 28. Sixty Corsairs and Hellcats participated in the December 27 sweep. They arrived just as the survivors of a Japanese airstrike against Cape Gloucester returned. The Japanese, who had lost seven out of 78 fighters sent during the Cape Gloucester attack, lost another seven in the ensuing melee. The Americans lost one. Twenty-eight Corsairs returned the next day. This time the Japanese got the advantage, sandwiching the Marines between two large groups of Zeroes.

First fighter sweep, December 17, 1943

The opening of the Torokina fighter strip permitted single-engine fighters to reach Rabaul. Major Gregory Boyington wanted to mark its opening with a fighter sweep over Rabaul. Although it was originally intended as a Marine-only activity, everyone else wanted to join in, too. When the sweep was flown on December 17, 80 aircraft participated – US Navy Hellcats, USMC Corsairs, and RNZAF Kittyhawks. The plan was for the Kittyhawks to come in first at 15,000ft to lure up the Japanese, with the Hellcats covering the Kittyhawks from above, and the Corsairs above the Hellcats.

The attempt at coordination fell apart while launching so many aircraft from one airstrip. Twenty Kittyhawks pressed on without waiting for the rest. Around 40 Zeroes from Lakunai and Tobera airfields took off to intercept the Kiwis. An aerial brawl took place in which two Zeroes and two Kittyhawks were downed. One Zero was shot down by Wing Commander Trevor O. Freeman, leader of the New Zealand contingent. In turn his Kittyhawk was hit in the engine and crashed.

A more spectacular incident occurred when Flyer 1st Class Masajiro Kawato collided with Flight Lieutenant John O. McFarland's Kittyhawk. Kawato was making a head-on pass at the Kittyhawk. Neither pilot was willing to break off and expose his aircraft to enemy fire. The two planes touched wings when Kawato tried to pull away. Kawato's Zero swung into McFarland's fuselage, striking it behind the pilot's compartment. Both pilots successfully bailed out and landed safely.

It was the second collision for Kawato, then 18. The previous month he had deliberately rammed an enemy fighter after running out of ammunition. McFarland, taken prisoner, died before the war ended. Kawato survived the war, leaving Rabaul when the aircraft were withdrawn. He eventually moved to the United States.

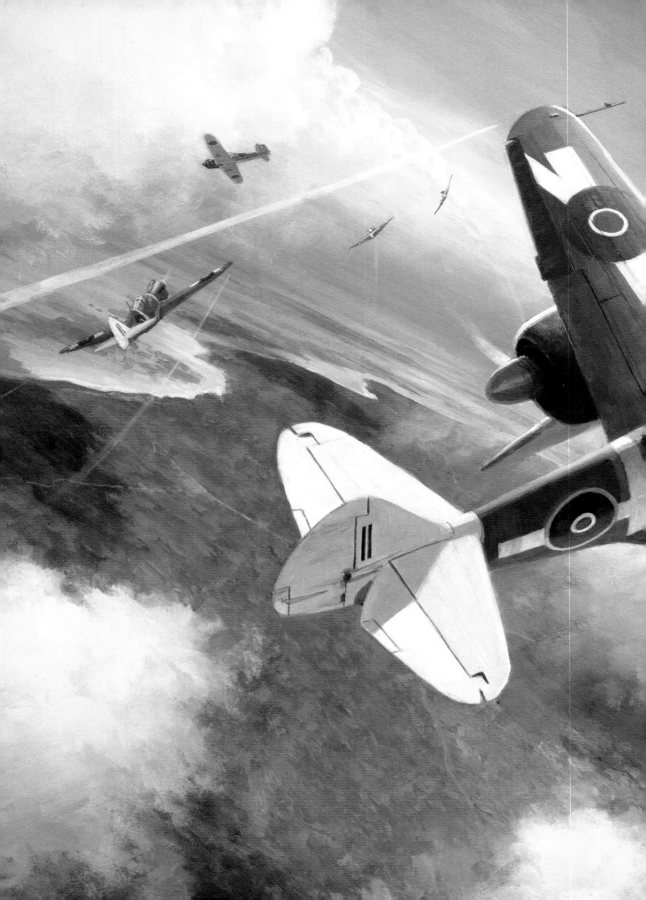

Whether under the Army name B-24 or the Navy designation PB4Y, the Liberator played an important role during the Rabaul campaign. These PB4Ys are on a patrol in the Southwest Pacific and were used for high-level bombing. (USNHHC)

Three Corsairs were shot down, but so were three Zeroes, with two others badly damaged.

Rain washed out operations on December 29 and a scheduled fighter sweep on December 30. However, 36 Liberators, escorted by 20 Hellcats and 20 Corsairs, bombed Rabaul. One B-24 was lost on the raid, hit by antiaircraft fire. No air combat occurred. Another bombing raid took place on January 1. This time, the 15 B-24s and 68 escorting fighters met heavy fighter opposition. A further 40 *Reisen* had been sent to Rabaul from Truk, manned by veteran pilots. One B-24 was shot down, and two others badly damaged. One of these two made an emergency landing at Torokina, where it and a Corsair were destroyed in a runway collision.

Two more fighter sweeps took place on January 2 and 3. Both were instigated by Boyington, eager to score a 26th and 27th kill before his tour ended. Making 26 allowed

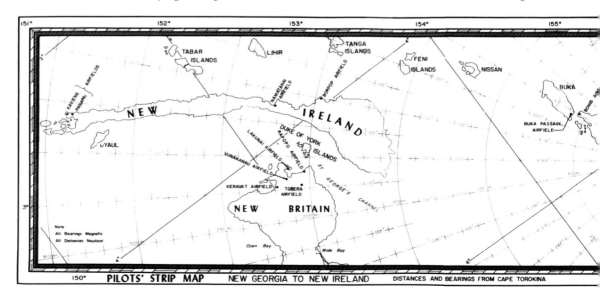

To further isolate Rabaul, United States Navy aircraft hit Kavieng on December 25, 1943. Two Japanese minesweepers pictured are under attack by US Navy carrier planes. (Note the F6F Hellcat between the two transports.) (USNHHC)

Boyington to tie Eddie Rickenbacker's World War I record of 26 aircraft shot down. More would exceed it, making Boyington America's ace-of-aces. Forty-eight US fighters flew the first sweep and 44 the second. The two sweeps managed to lure plenty of Zeroes into the air; 80 on the 2nd and 70 on the 3rd. The Japanese lost two fighters on each day, including one shot down by Boyington on January 3. However, the United States also lost two Corsairs on January 3, including one flown by Boyington. He spent the rest of the war a POW.

Boyington's loss marked a change in the tempo of the air war over Rabaul. For three weeks, the primary focus had been on fighter duels. It was a period emphasizing the "ace race" – where individual performance by fighter pilots was tracked as if they were athletes in a sports competition. While Boyington remains the best known fighter ace, there were others in the race. Joe Foss had also racked up 26 kills around Guadalcanal in 1942. Marion Carl, flying at the same time as Boyington, was credited with 18½, most the previous year but two in December 1943 at Rabaul. Robert Hanson would be credited with 25 kills

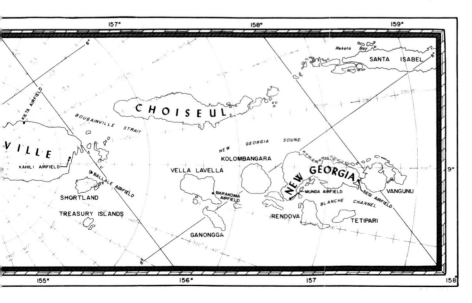

A pilot's strip map showing the route from Bougainville to Rabaul. Centered on Torokina, but usable with Piva, this would have been carried by pilots in single-engine aircraft making the long flight over the St George's Channel. (AC)

between November 1943 and February 1944. Foss, Boyington, and Hanson all received Medals of Honor for their performances.

The fame and promotion accompanying a successful fighter record led to an overemphasis on individual performance. It led many to exaggerate and some to falsify their claims. There were genuine reasons to overclaim. In the heat of combat it was easy to mistake damaging an aircraft for destroying it. American pilots assumed that if the engine of a Japanese aircraft started smoking, it was going to crash. But low octane gasoline and poor engine maintenance often caused Japanese aircraft to smoke heavily even when the engine was undamaged. However, some pilots, including Hanson, almost certainly lied about kills. Many of his claimed kills occurred when he was alone, having shaken off his wingman – and occasionally exceeded the total number of Japanese losses on that day.

Nor were the Allied pilots alone in exaggerating claims. For every false claim made by Allied pilots, Japanese pilots made ten. While Japanese pilots did not track individual scores, squadron scores were closely followed. Unit honor demanded their unit outperform rivals. Additionally when pilots were shot down, they would be credited with kills to honor their deaths.

Yet despite the exaggerations, the Allied air offensive was wearing down Rabaul. One last fighter sweep was flown on January 5, when Lightnings and Corsairs mixed it up with 33 Zeroes. Two Zeroes and two P-38s were shot down. But the tempo of the air war over Rabaul was about to change once again. On January 6, the bomber strip at Piva became operational. Rabaul was now within range of Allied light and medium bombers. Another 250 combat aircraft could reach Rabaul: tactical bombers capable of saturating Rabaul's airfields.

Rabaul encircled: January 7–February 27, 1944

When Torokina opened for business it began as a place to top off fuel tanks. Fighters staged from bases further south in the Solomons, and landed at Torokina to refuel before heading off to Rabaul. Once done they would land at Torokina to have enough fuel for the leg home. As time passed, more base facilities were added. By the last week of December pilots would fly up to Torokina in the evening, sleep in cots at newly built barracks, and fly off for Rabaul at dawn. By January the ground elements of the fighter squadrons using Torokina were relocating to Bougainville, and it was becoming a permanent home.

The Piva bomber strip on Bougainville served as an emergency strip as early as December 19, 1943. This photo shows the first aircraft to use the strip, an SBD Dauntless, landing as the Seabees building it watch. It became operational on January 10, 1944. (USNHHC)

When Piva Uncle was declared operational on January 6, the same pattern was followed. Piva Uncle then had a runway, taxiways and revetments, fueling facilities – and not much else. Light and medium bombers (mostly light bombers, since B-25s could reach Rabaul from Munda) would launch at dawn from their bases, land at Piva, refuel, and continue their mission.

The first such mission was flown January 7, 1944. SBDs left Munda for Rabaul, stopping at Piva. There they picked up an escort of Hellcats. The target was Tobera airfield, but it was socked in by rain. They hit the alternate: the Japanese radar station at Cape St George on the southern tip of New Ireland. Seventy Zeroes intercepted the flight. Three Hellcats and four SBDs were shot down. The radar station stayed on-line and the Japanese lost no fighters.

The next mission, on January 9, proved more successful – and an indication of things to come. Sixteen TBFs and 24 SBDs hit Tobera. The Japanese response was ferocious. Despite this, the Dauntlesses systematically worked over the antiaircraft positions. Then, at medium altitudes, the Avengers dropped 2,000lb bombs on the paved runway. Although the Japanese were able to shoot down three escorting fighters and one SBD, Tobera was temporarily shut down by the raid. It was the first time any Rabaul airbase was shut down due to bomb damage, even if it was temporary.

This was followed up on January 11 by another mission first: a low-level attack on Vunakanau by Army B-25s from the Solomons. Like the Fifth Air Force Mitchells, these airplanes had eight fixed forward-firing .50-caliber machine guns. The weather gods again favored Japan. Only half of the Mitchells found the target, but they damaged eight parked Japanese aircraft.

Then on January 14, General Ralph Mitchell, who commanded Comairsols, sent his aircraft against Lakunai, Rabaul's most heavily defended target. B-24s led off the attack, making a nighttime raid on the airfield on January 13/14. The day's second raid was made by B-25s, which attacked targets on New Ireland. Then 16 TBFs and 36 SBDs battled their way to Lakunai. They had company from the time they neared New Ireland until they reached the target and back down the St George's Channel. The Japanese had sent up 84 fighters. They had previously met the B-25s over New Ireland, and followed the Dauntlesses and Avengers up the St George's Channel.

Piva allowed light bombers, such as these TBF Avengers taxiing to take off for Rabaul, to reach the Gazelle Peninsula. Avengers and SBD dive bombers soon began making daily appearances over Rabaul. (AC)

ABOVE The *Narato Maru*, displacing 7,150 tons, was an early victim of Piva-based bombers. It was beached to prevent it from sinking after it had been bombed in Keravia Bay during a January raid mounted from Piva. (AC)

RIGHT By the end of February Comairsols bombardment had cratered the paved portions of all four airfields with improved surfaces. The runways at Rapopo (shown here) and Tobera were so badly damaged that these two fields were abandoned. (AC)

The bombers were well-guarded by fighter cover. RNZAF Kittyhawks flew close cover, while P-38s and F4Us gave top cover. As long as the formation held tight, the Japanese failed to press the attack against the bombers, although they fenced with the escort. Two bombers were lost before reaching Lakunai; one to a mid-air collision and one to antiaircraft fire. When the Allied aircraft finally arrived, clouds shielded Lakunai. The bombers switched to ships in Simpson Harbor. The Avengers carried 2,000lb bombs, limiting their effectiveness. Regardless, they landed hits on the 15,400-ton-displacement oiler *Naruto,* and the destroyer *Matsukaze. Naruto* was beached and later refloated. Five other ships were damaged. In addition to the two bombers lost, four fighters were shot down. The Japanese lost three.

Comairsols revisited Simpson Harbor and Blanche Bay three days later, on January 17. This time shipping was the primary target. At least five ships were sunk for a total of 30,000 tons: *Komaki Maru, Kosei Maru, Yamayuri Maru, Hakkai Maru,* and *Iwate Maru.* One ship had ten aircraft for the garrison aboard which had not been unloaded and were lost.

The attack was costly. Twelve Comairsols airplanes were lost: eight P-38s and an F6F, an F4U, a TBF and an SBD. Two B-25s and three Corsairs were lost two days later attacking Vunakanau. The price was worth it, however. Rabaul was beginning to cost the Japanese too much shipping. While the Imperial High Command was willing to absorb those losses for a while, they could not afford that rate of attrition for long.

Things got worse for the Japanese in the final ten days of January. The weather improved on January 21, providing a long period of clear weather. The Dauntless and Avenger squadrons had also transferred to Piva. Staging from the bases in the southern Solomons meant that raids over Rabaul predictably arrived at noon. Flying out of Piva gave a much wider arrival window, forcing Japanese fighters to remain airborne longer. Mitchell sent his aircraft over almost daily, sometimes mounting two or three different raids on the same day. American losses were brutal. Between January 23 and January 30, 23 planes were shot down. Japanese losses were worse. Over the same period they reported 37 aircraft downed. Thirteen were lost on January 23 alone.

By late January, Rabaul was running out of aircraft. Standard levels of replacements failed to maintain air group strength. On January 25 Admiral Koga ordered the 2nd Carrier Division to Rabaul. Made up of the air groups of three aircraft carriers at Truk, *Junyo, Hiyo,* and *Rhuyo,* this force added 62 Zeroes, 18 D3A Vals, and 18 B5N Kates. All but 20 of the remaining Zeroes, and a handful of the other aircraft of the Sixth Air Attack Force, then at Rabaul, were withdrawn to Truk, along with all but 40 pilots. The withdrawn survivors were allowed to recuperate or sent to training squadrons as instructors.

While this brought a respite for the relieved pilots, for the pilots sent to or retained at Rabaul the tempo was increasing. Between January 25 and January 31, Comairsols conducted daily raids against targets in the Gazelle Peninsula, again conducting two or three separate attacks in one day. They mixed up the targets. One day they would hit shipping in Blanche Bay and Simpson Harbor. The next day they would hit one or more airfields. Then they would attack targets in Rabaul city.

Nor were they making a single type of attack. During that period Tobera was hit by dive bombers, then high-altitude B-24s, followed by B-25s strafing or dropping bombs between 1,000ft and 5,000ft. Lakunai and Vunakanau were hit by daylight attacks at high, medium, and low altitudes, followed up by night bombings by B-24s. These would drop flares, both to illuminate the target and to keep the pilots and ground crew awake, and deprived of sleep.

The attacks were just as relentless in the first week of February. Weather compelled a two-day break at the beginning of the month, but Allied air forces returned on February 3. By February 7, nine separate airstrikes had been made, three each on Lakunai, Vunakanau, and Tobera.

These were sizable raids. On January 26, nearly 100 fighters and over 50 SBDs attacked Lakunai, targeting its antiaircraft guns. On January 28, nearly 200 aircraft hit multiple targets. On January 29, 100 aircraft were sent against Tobera. On February 6, 80 bombers and 110 fighters were sent against Lakunai. Only night attacks were smaller. They numbered between one and 20 aircraft.

The attacks quickly wore down Rabaul's air garrison. The Japanese met each raid by scrambling 35–85 fighters, often supplementing the fighters with D4Y1s to drop phosphorus bombs on Allied formations. Yet these aircraft were finding an environment simply too saturated with enemy aircraft. Allied bomber formations were protected by such large numbers of escorts, the Japanese fighters could not stop the bombers from reaching their targets. While the Japanese did succeed in shooting down Allied fighters during each mission, their losses in the air equaled or exceeded the number of aircraft they managed to down.

Nor were Japanese aircraft losses limited to aerial combat. The airfield raids were destroying aircraft on the ground. Not in the wholesale numbers of the October raids – too few Japanese aircraft were left for that. Yet each raid managed to destroy or disable between four and 20 aircraft on the ground. After two weeks of intensive bombing Japanese ground losses were approaching triple digits. Additionally, damage was not confined to aircraft. Each raid destroyed hangers, maintenance shops, and barracks. This reduced the ability of the Japanese to repair damaged aircraft or maintain undamaged fighters. A *Reisen* lost because its engine had quit due to bad spark plugs was just as gone as one lost to a Corsair's bullets.

The ability to defend an airbase was also reduced by every crater a 2,000lb bomb left on a runway. The Japanese still had plenty of POW laborers to level the runway and fill in the bomb craters. But the paved surfaces were being replaced with crushed coral which left soft spots after the frequent tropical rains. Operational accidents increased as a result.

Dive bombing also proved hellishly effective against aerodrome antiaircraft positions. The hits only occasionally destroyed a gun. Bombing destroyed only one-quarter of the antiaircraft artillery on Rabaul. The attacks proved deadly to their crews, however. After being bombed several times the survivors became more interested in reaching cover than hitting enemy aircraft.

Marine PBJ Mitchells headed towards Rabaul fly over the invasion convoy on course to invade the Green Islands, the day before the February 15 landing. (LOC)

Aircraft losses could be replaced only with difficulty. The 2nd Carrier Division represented Japan's last available air reserves. Ironically, the Japanese had nearly 150 replacement aircraft at Truk in late January and early February. Shipped from Japan in crates, they required assembly at Truk before they could be sent to Rabaul. But there were too few aircraft mechanics at Truk to assemble the crated aircraft quickly enough to replace losses.

The Allies could replace their losses. They could also reinforce what totals they did have. The second week of February saw yet another uptick in Allied activity with an increase in the number of attacks and the number of aircraft committed to each attack. On February 10, the Allies filled the air over the Gazelle Peninsula with 275 aircraft – nearly twice the strength of the Japanese air garrison.

After February 12, Mitchell began adding P-39s to the mix escorting bombers. The Airacobra, slow and unmaneuverable, was outclassed by the Zero. But it carried a 37mm cannon which worked magnificently strafing ground targets. By mid-February the Zero posed so little threat that including the P-39 improved Allied capabilities without risking disproportionate losses.

Bad as things were for Japan by the second week of February, things got still worse during the third week. On February 15, the Allies invaded the Green Islands, a small atoll east of New Ireland. Reconnaissance flights made in late January revealed that the islands were virtually undefended by the Japanese, and possessed terrain capable of holding an airfield. They were only 115 miles from Rabaul. An invasion force was hastily assembled and on February 15, two brigades from the 3rd New Zealand Division were landed.

Kusaka attempted to break up the landing by attacking the invasion fleet the night before it took place. He sent 32 D3As and B5Ns to bomb the fleet. Twelve bombers were shot down on February 14, and 15 more lost when unescorted D3As ran into fighter cover over the fleet on the next day. Japanese resistance was quickly overcome – there were fewer than 150 soldiers in the garrison, and the Kiwis had 5,800. The Seabees moved in and built an airfield on Nissan Island. By March 16, aircraft from Nissan were bombing Kavieng.

Then on February 16 and 17 Truk was hit by a massive airstrike launched by US Navy aircraft carriers. Operation *Hailstone* saw Truk worked over by the aircraft of five fleet carriers and five light carriers. The attack temporarily closed down Truk as a conduit of supplies to Rabaul.

Finally, to add insult to injury, after sunset on February 17 five US Navy destroyers bombarded Rabaul. The bombardment went on until after midnight on February 18. Using

Attack from above

On February 10, 1944, 59 Dauntless dive bombers and 24 Avengers, escorted by 99 fighters, pasted Vunakanau airfield. The fighter escort prevented Japanese interference with the bombers. The Avengers dropped bombs on the runway and facilities, while the Dauntlesses methodically took out the antiaircraft batteries.

There are few things more terrifying than being dive-bombed, especially when you know – as the crews of the antiaircraft guns knew – the dive bomber is aiming at you. The airplane heads straight for you. You watch it swell in size as it approaches the drop point. You cannot tell whether the bomb is going to hit or miss, because even if it does miss the geometry makes it appear it is heading right at you. Making things worse, a dive bomber is a difficult target to hit. It comes straight at you, offering just a narrow head-on target: the width of its wings and the diameter of its fuselage is all that is visible. If you do hit it, the wreck is likely to land on or near you.

Paradoxically, a large antiaircraft gun is even less likely to hit a dive bomber than a smaller-caliber antiaircraft gun. The large gun does not aim directly at an airplane. It aims at a spot in the sky where it expects the airplane to be. The shell is fused to fire at a specific altitude. This works well with level bombers, but the altitude of a dive bomber is constantly changing until it hits the drop point. Guess wrong, and the shell harmlessly bursts above or below the target. And on this day, there were more dive bombers than there were antiaircraft guns – nearly twice as many bombers as gun positions.

All the targeted crew could do was fire as fast as they could and hope the shells were fused properly. On several occasions antiaircraft crews broke under the strain.

Having achieved air superiority, the Allies turned to Rabaul city. These Maine PBJs are over the Crater Peninsula heading to Rabaul. Flak is still heavy, indicating that this photo was taken at the beginning of this phase. (USNHHC)

rain squalls for cover and radar-guided gunfire, the destroyers dropped 3,868 5in artillery rounds into Rabaul city over Crater Peninsula. They then retired south, firing 15 torpedoes at shipping in Blanche Bay as they passed. The torpedo attack did relatively little damage, but indicated the deterioration of Japanese air power around Rabaul. US Navy destroyers would make two more such attacks before February ended, with the Japanese powerless to stop them. The biggest hazard these destroyers would face was friendly aircraft. Returning from the third raid they were attacked by overeager Allied aircraft, thrilled at a rare opportunity to attack a naval target at sea. Fortunately, the attackers were out of practice, and missed.

As the Japanese air garrison grew weaker, Allied air strikes became bolder. Believing that Lakunai, Vunakanau, and Tobera were on the ropes, Comairsols turned attention onto Rapopo airfield and the warehouses around it, and on the remaining shipping in the harbor. Rapopo field was hit on February 14, 21, and 24. At the end of the third raid its runways were cratered and buildings were ruined. Large strikes hit the remaining shipping in the harbor on February 17 and 22. Six ships were sunk, most in Keravia Bay. The tonnage was half of what it had been in the January 17 attack. The ships still at Rabaul were smaller. On February 19 a massive airstrike was made on Rabaul city.

The Japanese kept challenging the Allied air raids, and kept losing aircraft. Even as late as February 19 35–50 Zeroes were scrambled to intercept that day's raid. It was the last serious attempt to meet the Allies in the air. Imperial command decided to pull the plug two days later. A partial evacuation had started in January evacuating non-essential personnel, such as the "comfort girls." On February 21 critical personnel including 350 ground personnel for the *rikko* units were shipped out. Most never reached Truk. The homebound ships were sunk by submarines and aircraft. No more freighters were sent to Rabaul.

Between February 19 and 23 all airworthy aircraft departed for Truk. In October, when the Allied air offensive started, there were 300 aircraft at Rabaul. Only 24 G4Ms, 40 A6Ms, 21 D3As, 4 D4Y1s, and 11 B5Ns flew home in February. Rabaul was on its own.

Oblivion: February 28–March 28, 1944

Following the departure of the Japanese air fleet from Rabaul the garrison was effectively isolated. Sea traffic, except for barges, ceased. The Allies had total control of the air and water in the seas around New Britain and New Ireland. If Comairsols aircraft failed to sink ships heading into or out of Rabaul, US submarines or even US Navy surface warships would.

The only way into and out of Rabaul was by air. Even that connection was tenuous. Allied airfields were beginning to ring Rabaul. If Rabaul were viewed as the center of a clock face, by late February the Allies had airfields from 3 o'clock (Nissan on the Green Islands) to 8 o'clock (Cape Gloucester). Japanese aircraft could still escape Allied fighters once away from the immediate vicinity of Rabaul by flying due north from Rabaul for an hour or so. Flying a straight-line path risked interception from the Green Islands. Once clear of the range of Allied fighters, aircraft could reach the dubious safety of Truk.

Flying into Rabaul was a different story. Multiple daily raids meant incoming Japanese aircraft were likely to arrive in the middle of a fighter sweep. Despite the risk, General Hideki Tojo, Japan's Prime Minister, made his first (and only) visit to Rabaul in late February. He was accompanied by the Minister of the Navy, Admiral Yaichiro Shibata, and the Chief of the Imperial Japanese Navy General Staff, Osami Nagano. The three held meetings with Imamura and Kusaka to plan the future defense of Rabaul. There really was nothing the trio could tell Rabaul's commanders, other than hold to the last, something Imamura and Kusaka intended even before the visit.

There were still a handful of Japanese aircraft at Rabaul, but far fewer than the Allies realized. Aerial reconnaissance photos taken on February 25 showed 33 aircraft. Most of these were unflyable wrecks. There were around ten flyable Zeroes still in the Gazelle Peninsula and a few bombers. All had been patched together from bits and pieces of other damaged aircraft. These were concealed in caves, and would take to the air singly, just to prove the Japanese were still there and still fighting. These efforts were meaningless pinpricks when related against the hundreds of Allied combat aircraft flying over Rabaul daily.

The Allies were throwing more aircraft into the fight each week, too. The Marines, always eager for a bigger role, discovered unused B-25s in the rear echelons. The USAAF was short of pilots and aircrew. Earlier, the Marines had created fighter squadrons to use

Rabaul was further isolated on February 29, 1944 when Allied forces landed on the Admiralty Islands. Airfields on Los Negros cut off Rabaul, and supported further Allied offensives. By August 1945 the Los Negros airfields had grown into a major complex. (USNHHC)

Corsairs surplus to Navy needs. Now the Marines organized new Marine squadrons for the surplus Mitchells, providing pilots and crews for these PBJs – as the Marine Corps and Navy designated the B-25.

The ring around Rabaul closed a little tighter on February 29. On that day Allied forces landed on Los Negros Island in the Admiralties, a group of islands on the northwestern fringe of the Bismarck Sea. The first target was Momote aerodrome, a field painstakingly built by the occupying Japanese following their occupation of the Admiralties in 1942. It was captured on the day of landing. While the invasion of the Admiralties created another brick in the wall being built around Rabaul, isolating Rabaul was not the main reason for the invasion.

Seealder Harbor was the attraction. Although Rabaul was to be bypassed, the Allies still needed a naval base north of New Britain to support future operations against Japan. Seealder Harbor, 15 miles long and 4 miles wide, was not as good as Simpson Harbor, but it was good enough. The Japanese had 100,000 soldiers guarding Rabaul; their garrison at the Admiralties totaled around 3,000. The Allies soon had control of Los Negros and the eastern part of neighboring Manus Island. They also had control of the land around Seealder Harbor and held the two Japanese-built airfields. Momote airfield eventually became a major Allied airfield.

Meanwhile the Allied air campaign against Rabaul continued unabated and gained momentum. It took a week for the Allies to realize Japanese aircraft were no longer challenging air raids. When they did, the Allies' emphasis shifted away from attacking the Gazelle Peninsula's airfields. The new priorities were the stores held in Rabaul, barges and other remaining craft in Rabaul's waters, and, finally, goods stockpiled in warehouses scattered throughout the Gazelle Peninsula.

The absence of Japanese air resistance left the Allies with a surplus of fighters. The solution was to use aircraft less capable of air-to-air combat as fighter-bombers. This had started earlier with P-39s, although they were used primarily as strafers. Starting on February 23, P-38s and P-40s added bomb racks and began carrying one 1,000lb or two 500lb bombs on each mission.

Mitchell and his staff divided Rabaul into 14 sectors, and broke each sector into two or three parts. A systematic bombing campaign was planned where each part would be attacked in turn until destroyed. Once this was done, the raids would concentrate on the next sector until Rabaul was completely flattened.

The campaign started March 1. Wave after wave of bombers would hit a designated part of Rabaul each day. B-24s would bomb at high altitude. Army B-25s and Marine PBJs conducted medium-altitude level bombing. SBDs attacked antiaircraft positions to suppress the only resistance the Japanese could still make. In assembly-line fashion Comairsols burned out Rabaul. An average of 85 tons of bombs was dropped on Rabaul each day. By March 10, only 12 days after the start of the campaign, 60 percent of Rabaul had been flattened. A week later, two-thirds of the town was gone. By April 20, only 122 buildings were still standing.

Nor was the harbor neglected. By March 1, the only ships still in Simpson Harbor or Blanche Bay were the ones sunk earlier. No new shipping visited. There were still plenty of barges scattered about the two bodies of water – over 500. These were used to carry supplies to minor Japanese garrisons elsewhere in New Britain and the Solomons, or to ferry material from New Ireland to New Britain. Comairsols turned its attention to these, sinking over 200 barges in February and March. By then the survivors were either scattered elsewhere or hidden in caves, coming out only at night.

Even before the bombing of Rabaul proper ceased, supply dumps, warehouses, repair shops, communications facilities, power plants, and sawmills in the rest of the Gazelle Peninsula were targeted. As late as January 1944, most of Rabaul's supplies and infrastructure were above ground; supplies were stored in unprotected warehouses or lightly built buildings or even tents. Supplies had flowed in faster than they could be properly stored throughout 1942 and the first half of 1943. So much had been brought in that the Japanese seized virtually every available existing building within the Gazelle Peninsula for their own use, and built 29 sawmills to create lumber for new structures from the native timber. At their peak they could produce 185,000 board-feet of lumber each week.

By October 1943 buildings aggregating 3 million square feet of area were within the city of Rabaul and another 1.7 million square feet of buildings scattered over the rest of the Gazelle Peninsula. These buildings and their contents began falling to bomb and blast from the inexorable Allied bombing campaign. Between January and March over 40 percent of the

Throughout the campaign land-based Marine SBD Dauntless dive bombers bombed antiaircraft positions, suppressing their fire. After the Japanese withdrew aircraft from Rabaul, antiaircraft artillery was the only means of resistance left to the Japanese. (AC)

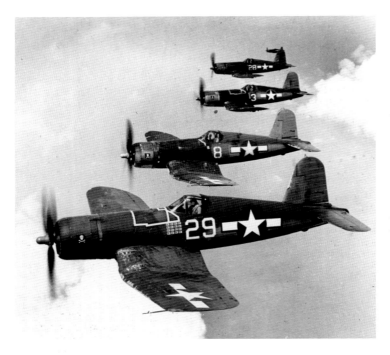

The "ace race" ended when Japanese aircraft departed, but fighter squadrons still supported the air offensive. These are Vought F4U-1A Corsair fighters of VF-17 in flight, in early March 1944. Aircraft 29 is flown by Ira Kepford, then the Navy's leading ace, with 16 kills. (USNHHC)

stockpiled food in Rabaul was destroyed by bombing, as was nearly one-third of the canteen and medical stores. Eighty percent of machinery in repair and machine shops was destroyed. One-third of the power plants were flattened. The Navy lost 750 tons of ammunition. The Army, better dispersed, only lost 5 percent of its ammunition. One-eighth of the gasoline stockpiled was similarly destroyed.

Most of these losses occurred between January and the first two weeks of March. As early as November 1943 the Japanese had realized their vulnerability to aerial assault, and had begun dispersing supplies and facilities. Much of their stores of goods went underground. The volcanic rock of New Britain was easily carved yet extremely resistant to bombs. The Japanese had plenty of labor available for digging. The POWs and conscripted civilians that Japan had moved to Rabaul stopped making runways and started carving caves.

Between November and March a network of underground storage facilities sprouted beneath the Gazelle Peninsula's surface. Warehouses moved underground, as did repair shops, communications facilities, barracks, and hospitals. Sometimes the facilities were rough, with bare rock walls. Other facilities, including command centers and radio rooms were paneled with wood ceilings, walls, and floors.

The Japanese built underground shelters for antiaircraft guns and spotlights, as well. After a position was hit, the gun or spotlight in it would be moved to a nearby location, where a cave would be dug. The item would wait in the cave until needed. It would then be rolled to position (typically rails were added), used briefly, and then rolled back to shelter. After a few minutes had passed, it would be deployed again.

Allied aircraft also hit the road network in the absence of other targets. As a result, most truck and automobile movement was done at night. Vehicles that had to travel during daylight hours followed roads concealed from air observation (13 percent of the road network was completely hidden and another 20 percent partially hidden) or along roads which had air lookouts every 500–1,000 yards. If an aircraft were spotted, the driver would be warned, and hide under cover until the danger had passed.

By March everything of value that remained in the Gazelle Peninsula, except food and fuel, had been moved underground. Food, especially rice and grains, quickly spoiled in the damp confines of the cave system. Rice was stored in open pits, concealed by vegetation. Fuel, similarly, was concealed by jungle.

Most of the stores the Allies did destroy were eradicated while still stored above ground. Had Mitchell shifted to bombing supplies a few weeks earlier than he did, up to half of all supplies, fuel, food, and ammunition on Rabaul would have been destroyed. Instead, the Japanese had sufficient supplies to last out the war.

The bombing campaign conducted in late February and March did not destroy the Rabaul garrison, or significantly reduce the fighting capabilities of Japanese ground forces or coastal defenses. What it did do was render Rabaul impotent. On March 9 unescorted bombing missions over Rabaul began. By the end of March Japanese forces in Rabaul could not project power further than their artillery could shoot and that only feebly. It ensured that even if Japan could reopen an air bridge or a sea route to Rabaul it would be a long time before it could be used as a base for offensive operations.

As March progressed, the chances of Japan reopening a road to Rabaul dimmed markedly. On March 8, the airfield at Nissan opened. This put Kavieng within range of Allied single-engine fighters. A Fifth Air Force raid had already devastated Kavieng in mid-February, all but closing it. On March 16, Nissan field mounted its first major raid against Kavieng. SBDs and TBFs escorted by Allied aircraft replicated the work they had been doing at Rabaul against a new target. Kavieng experienced the same treatment that Rabaul had suffered over the previous month.

The ability to cover Kavieng with Corsairs, Hellcats, Kittyhawks, and even Airacobras meant that Kavieng could no longer be used even to ferry aircraft to Rabaul. The only route left was a nonstop flight to or from Truk, with a long swim home if the engines failed during the journey. Soon half the Kittyhawks and most of the Airacobras were stationed at Nissan.

The final bricks in the wall being built around Rabaul were placed on March 20, when Allied troops landed on Emirau. This was a small island 100 miles northwest of Kavieng. It had two primary virtues: it could hold an airfield and was believed to have a very small Japanese garrison.

Originally Allied war plans had called for an invasion at Kavieng too. Its airfield would close the ring around Rabaul, and its harbor could substitute for Simpson Harbor. But Seealder Harbor, taken when the Admiralties were seized, was a perfectly adequate

The bombardment of Rabaul continued for two months, but by the third week much of the city had already been flattened. This attack took place on March 22. The eastern side of the city is destroyed, including the portion of the city containing the waterfront pictured in the previous Rabaul photo. (USNHHC)

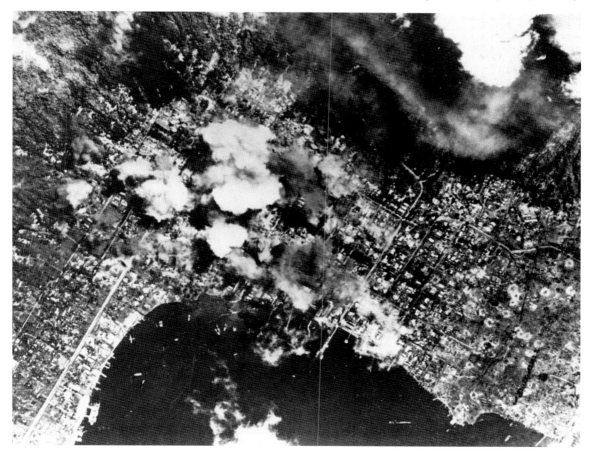

replacement for Simpson Harbor and was better placed than either Kavieng or Rabaul to support future Allied movement on the road to Japan. That left the airfield as a reason to land at Kavieng. Kavieng was heavily garrisoned, however. To take it would require committing two infantry divisions, the 3rd Marine Division and 40th Infantry Division, backed up by the 4th Marine Regiment.

The Green Islands showed that the main reason to take an island was to use it to hold an airfield. The whole Rabaul campaign demonstrated that physical occupation of a strongly held enemy position was unnecessary if air superiority could be achieved. At virtually the last minute the invasion of Kavieng was canceled, and Emirau substituted. Japanese garrisons at both Kavieng and Mussau (north of Emirau) were bypassed. The landing at Emirau was virtually unopposed.

Nimitz had ordered a bombardment of Kavieng's port and airfield preparatory to a landing at Kavieng. The switch was made so late that the four old battleships assigned to do the bombardment were already in the area. In the belief that it would be a good diversion, the bombardment took place as planned on March 20. Meanwhile the 4th Marine Brigade was making an unopposed landing at Emirau. There were no Japanese on the island.

Airfield construction was begun on March 31. An emergency strip was available by April 14. The airfield was operational by May 2 – the leisurely pace a result of the winding down of the Rabaul campaign.

By March 31 there was no question that the Allies had succeeded in neutralizing Rabaul. Its air garrison had been reduced to a handful of aircraft. Rabaul city had been flattened. The garrison had turned into subterranean and nocturnal creatures. They lived and worked underground and generally emerged from their caves only at night.

Endgame: April 1944–August 1945

By mid-April 90 percent of the buildings in Rabaul had been destroyed. The Allies ended large-scale bombing raids for a lack of targets. They continued bombing the three largest Japanese airbases, Lakunai, Vunakanau, and Tobera, initially every week and then every other week, to make sure they could not be made operational. Rapopo and Keravat were recognized as abandoned, and rarely attacked after June 1944.

With a lack of conventional objectives, the Allied flyers sought more unusual targets. In June and July of 1944 they went after the crops the Japanese were raising. Mechanics fixed sprayers to Avenger torpedo bombers, and put 150-gallon fuel tanks into the bomb bay.

These aircraft then flew over fields releasing diesel fuel on the plants, killing them. Similarly, Japanese attempts to harvest fish in the waters around Rabaul ended with their fishing boats attacked and sunk – along with anything else found still floating, right down to the smallest rowboat. These attacks were intended to force the Japanese to draw down stored food, since outside resupply was impossible.

There was also dusk-to-dawn harassment of Japanese airfields. A single medium bomber – a B-25 or more typically a Marine PBJ – would circle an airfield starting at sunset. It dropped a single 100lb bomb every five minutes or so. After 90 minutes, that aircraft would be relieved by a new one, and the process repeated. This bombing was intended to deprive the garrison of sleep. Plenty of Allied aircraft were available, and a single airfield could be covered for the night by fewer than a dozen bombers.

Vunakanau was the biggest airfield in New Britain in September 1943. A year later it had been destroyed by Allied bombing. Every building was gone, its aircraft destroyed, and its concrete runway reduced to rubble. (AC)

As June 1944 passed into July and August, the Allies began drawing down forces, sending squadrons and troops to more active theaters. The Fifth Air Force moved out into northwestern New Guinea and the Philippines. The Thirteenth Air Force moved out of the Solomons area, relocating at the Admiralties. Responsibility for Rabaul gradually shifted to RAAF and RNZAF squadrons left in the Mandate territories.

The United States still flew combat missions over Rabaul, using it as an area for newly formed squadrons to gain combat experience, and as a place to test new weapons. In October 1944 the US Navy used Rabaul to combat-test remotely piloted bombs – drone aircraft in today's language. The results were underwhelming.

Flying over Rabaul remained dangerous. The Japanese never ran short of ammunition, even by the war's end. Antiaircraft fire, sudden rain squalls, or mechanical problems could still bring down Allied aircraft up to the last month of the war. As late as January 1945 flak and weather combined to bring down eight Allied aircraft in a single mission.

Having lost control of the sky above and sea around the Gazelle Peninsula the garrison dug in to hold the ground around Rabaul. It had ample means to do so. While Allied bombing destroyed Rabaul's air facilities and its infrastructure and transportation network, for the most part it left Japanese ground weapons alone. Since the Allies had no intention to occupy the Gazelle Peninsula, destroying a truck was more important than destroying a tank. The truck could help the Japanese restore its airfields; a tank could not.

Between April and September of 1944 US troops swept east on New Britain, taking airfields at Talasea and Gatsama. In November 1944 Allied troops landed at Jacquinot Bay. The Australian 5th Infantry Division then pushed forward to the neck formed by Wide Bay and Open Bay at the entrance to the Gazelle Peninsula. They never pushed beyond that, content to isolate the Japanese there. For the Allies, leaving the Imperial Japanese Army troops penned up in Rabaul was simpler than capturing them. Functionally it was an open-air prisoner of war camp, with the inmates running it, and the jailers not obligated to feed, house, and clothe their charges. The Japanese waited for an invasion which never came.

Illness soared, and food remained short. The Allies never came close to starving Rabaul out, although rations were reduced. But even though few members of the garrison realistically expected relief, morale remained good. The Japanese on Rabaul did not sit by waiting for the war to end. Even after the withdrawal of most of the aircraft from Rabaul a few aircraft, several pilots, and most of the ground staff remained. From the wrecks, the Japanese pieced together enough parts to make a few flying aircraft. Parts were salvaged from unflyable aircraft and added to those which were lightly damaged. When parts were unavailable, new parts were manufactured. In some cases metal from wrecks was melted down and used to cast new parts.

This allowed the Japanese to keep a few aircraft flying. Not many, but enough to keep one or two fighters around to show Allied flyers that Japan was still in the game. In April 1945, a year after the Allies gained air superiority over Rabaul, and when the Admiralties had become a backwater base, two slapped-together B5N torpedo bombers launched a night raid on Seealder Harbor. Both aircraft managed to launch a torpedo. Both torpedoes hit. One of the two B5Ns disappeared after the attack. The other returned to Rabaul, where the pilot reported that an American aircraft carrier had been torpedoed and sunk. In reality the two torpedoes had been fired at a floating drydock, which could easily have been mistaken for an aircraft carrier in the dark. The drydock was only damaged.

That raid and other sorties mounted by Rabaul-based aircraft between May 1944 and August 1945 were just nuisances. They served to remind the Allies that the Japanese were still there. They were a far cry from the massive attacks flown by Rabaul's *rikko* only two years previously and only underscored the impotence of Japanese air power.

The Navy tested unmanned drones at Rabaul. This is an Interstate TDR-1 assault drone being prepared for the Rabaul attack. This photograph shows the bomb being hoisted into position and television guidance equipment inside the nose. The tests were unsuccessful. (USNHHC)

AFTERMATH AND ANALYSIS

The end finally came on September 6, 1945. The war ended three weeks earlier when Emperor Hirohito read the Imperial Rescript announcing Japan's surrender. Hostilities ceased on that day, and the Japanese on Rabaul freed the prisoners they held. But the Allied powers had to arrange to send forces to accept the formal surrender of the garrison, including arrangements to manage the expected 30,000 Japanese estimated to be in the garrison. Since New Britain was then part of an Australian mandate, Australian troops were sent to accept the surrender.

On September 6, the aptly named HMS *Vendetta*, a World War-I era "V"-class destroyer, steamed into Simpson Harbor to arrange the surrender. It was chosen because it had no further use and, should the Japanese attack, its loss would be relatively unimportant. *Vendetta* would be paid off in November and scuttled in July 1946. The next day a Royal Navy sloop took General Imamura and Admiral Kusaka to HMS *Glory*, a Colossus-class light aircraft carrier anchored in Kabanga Bay, a shallow inlet on the Gazelle Peninsula 7 miles southwest of Cape Gazelle. The Australians distrusted the Japanese too much to put an aircraft carrier within range of Japanese shore batteries.

The fight went out of the Japanese after their emperor ordered them to lay down their arms, however. Imamura and Kusaka signed the surrender document on *Glory*'s deck. Imamura, as senior officer, also surrendered his sword as required by the Australians as a further token of capitulation.

The Japanese, including those on outlying islands, numbered 140,000, nearly five times what the Australians expected. Since this was too many to guard, the Australians disarmed the garrison, and then directed the Japanese to organize and build camps to live in until they could be repatriated to Japan. The Japanese also had to feed themselves, a difficulty somewhat eased by remaining food stores and because no one attacked the crops they raised. Repatriation did not begin until May 1946 and was not complete until October, a year after the surrender was signed. Only then was the siege of Rabaul completely over.

Damage from fragmentation bombs or a near miss from a 1,000lb bomb made this Mitsubishi G3M at Rapopo inoperable. Its revetment became overgrown with vegetation between November 1943 and November 1945 when this picture was taken. (AC)

General Imamura presents his sword to Australian General Vernon Sturdee in a surrender ceremony on the deck of HMS *Glory*. Vice Admiral Kusaka stands next to Imamura. (AC)

Rabaul was the first campaign where air power was successfully used to deliberately isolate and neutralize a major stronghold to the point where occupation by ground forces was neither attempted nor necessary. Air power had already become a critical element to victory during World War II. Prior to the decision to bypass Rabaul there were numerous campaigns where airpower allowed a land army to defeat another land army, including Poland in 1939 and France in 1940.

In some senses the Japanese campaigns in Malaya (including the capture of Singapore) and the Philippines were prototypes for the Allies' Rabaul campaign. In both cases air power, sometimes assisted by sea power, isolated and immobilized larger enemy land forces. Large enemy armies were trapped by absolute domination of the skies above the army. The difference was that at the end of both campaigns the victor concluded the campaign by land invasion.

This was also the pattern for early Allied offensives in both the European and Pacific theaters. Air power isolated and immobilized an enemy stronghold, allowing ground forces to destroy it. This pattern was followed in the Solomon Islands and especially New Guinea in 1942–43. Rabaul broke from past policy because it was recognized that once a large garrison was isolated and immobilized by airpower it could be ignored thereafter. Physical occupation by ground forces was unnecessary, and cost casualties.

Rabaul was not won through airpower alone. It was an aerial victory, but it was an aerial victory that would have been impossible without appropriate support from naval and land forces. The Allies won because they had the military and naval capability to gain the necessary bases for their air forces, as well as the idea to do so. The Japanese by this point in the war lacked the flexibility or reserves to counter these moves.

The key to victory was air superiority. With air superiority everything became easier. Your forces could move faster because they did not have to fear air attack. The enemy was more likely to be observed, which allowed better estimation of its strengths and weaknesses. Your forces were less likely to be observed, which improved the chances of surprising your enemy. Most importantly air superiority allowed one side to isolate its opponent from supply. Without supply a 20th-century army could not move.

The key to achieving air superiority was having high-performance fighters available. In 1943–44 this meant single-engine fighters. There were effective twin-engine fighters; the P-38 was one example. But generally a single-engine fighter could outperform a twin-engine fighter from the same period. That the P-38 held its own against the Zero was more evidence of the impending obsolescence of the Zero than of the P-38's innate superiority over single-engine designs.

The drawback to single-engine fighters of 1943–44 was that they generally had much shorter range than did multi-engine aircraft. Air superiority could only be achieved within the narrow radius reached by single-engine fighters. The Japanese solution was long-range single-engine fighters, an objective achieved only through sacrificing all defensive capability and a lot of structural strength. The Allied solution was to place airfields close enough to their objective to allow shorter-ranged (but better-protected) single-engine aircraft to reach. Each approach had advantages and drawbacks – illustrated in the Rabaul campaign.

The main advantage of the Japanese approach was to permit concentration of force in a central location, such as Rabaul or Wewak. Japanese Zeroes stationed at Rabaul could escort bombers to Port Moresby or Guadalcanal. Since they were operating on interior lines, the Japanese could concentrate force at one location, while the Allies were forced to divide fighters between individual bases. This approach gave Japan a much smaller logistical footprint. The downside to the Japanese approach was that their fighters were fragile – a fragility which remained when they were forced to defend their bases and range was unimportant.

The advantage to the Allied approach was that it gave them much more capable fighters. Even less-capable early-war fighters like the P-40 or F4F Wildcat could meet Zeroes on relatively even terms due to their ability to absorb punishment. By 1943 the next generation of fighters, which in the Rabaul campaign included the F6F and F4U, dominated the

The Rabaul waterfront at the end of the war was a scene of devastation, with virtually every building destroyed, wharves wrecked, and ships beached. From top to bottom are the RAAF jetty, the Netherlands Line wharf, and the remains of the Burns-Phillips wharf. (AC)

The successful Allied bombing campaign forced the Japanese underground. Some facilities, including this Army radio station at Lat Latm, were contained in elaborate cave facilities. Boards paneled the walls, ceilings, and floor of this room. (AC)

Zero. The drawback to this approach was that superiority did not matter unless they were within range. This required building airfields – lots of airfields. The pattern of the Rabaul campaign was a leapfrog strategy where airfields were built increasingly close to Rabaul. In the Solomons the chain went Henderson Field (Guadalcanal) – Munda (New Georgia) – Bougainville (Torokina and Piva). A similar pattern was executed in New Guinea. Supporting the personnel to capture territory and run and protect the airfields, as well as supplying the material needed to build and maintain airfields, put a lot of strain on logistics.

Logistics ultimately proved the key to gaining air superiority and victory in the campaign. It was not just that the Allies had a bigger logistical base to work from, although they did. Rather the Allies made better use of the resources that they had than did the Japanese.

During the period of the Rabaul campaign the Southwest Pacific Theater, which included New Britain and Rabaul, had the lowest priority for manpower and equipment, well behind what was being sent to Europe and Africa, and behind the Central Pacific Theater. Realizing the scarcity of men and supplies and the difficulty in bringing either from the United States' West Coast, Allied leaders did their best to ensure that both were sent expeditiously, and that sufficient emphasis was placed on construction and maintenance assets.

Space was allocated for bulldozers and graders even if it meant forgoing extra tanks. Adequate numbers of mechanics and spare parts were sent to allow aircraft to be maintained. Maintenance was centralized to improve efficiency. Airfields could be built at a phenomenal pace – in as little as three weeks. The day after the Fifth Air Force launched its October 12 attack 95 percent of the B-25s and 80 percent of the B-24s and P-38s which flew that mission were ready to attack again the next day. They had been repaired (when necessary), serviced, refueled, and rearmed in a few hours' time. It was a remarkable demonstration of Allied maintenance capabilities, one routinely repeated during the campaign.

By contrast, the Japanese gave logistics a low priority, paying little attention to it, using slave labor wherever possible. At Rabaul most work involved with construction and supply handling was done by POWs, forced to labor without pay while living in shoddy barracks with inadequate food. They had no incentive to work hard. Many were motivated to conduct petty sabotage when they could do so without getting caught.

While Rabaul was stuffed with supplies delivered during 1942 and 1943, there was no organization to its storage. Supplies were dumped ashore where convenient, and left unprotected. Several offensive operations during the period were delayed due to the time it took to find necessary supplies and equipment. Nor was any effort put into dispersing or protecting supplies until November 1943, and dispersal was not complete until March 1944.

This inefficiency was not limited to Rabaul. The entire Japanese logistical, manufacturing, and maintenance chain was unresponsive and inefficient. Zero production was constricted due to difficulties in transporting aircraft from the factory, which required completed aircraft to be moved 20 miles by oxcart. Nor were there ever sufficient mechanics or facilities to service aircraft. Truk was the biggest Japanese base outside the Home Islands. Yet at a critical point during the defense of Rabaul 150 desperately needed Zeroes were sitting at Truk, crated up in packing containers from the factory. The Japanese had an insufficient number of mechanics to assemble the aircraft. Many were still unassembled when the US Navy attacked Truk in February 1944.

Another difference between the two sides was their attitude to technology. The Allies embraced it, while the Japanese often failed to appreciate it. This can most clearly be seen in the way both sides used radar. By mid-1943 the Allies not only had radar, they had assimilated it. Radar was common on naval warships, and used not only for early warning, but for gunnery. Airfields had radar, and both ships and land bases integrated radar into air defense, vectoring fighters to the enemy based on radar observation. Radar served as a force multiplier both in the air and in naval engagements.

Japan had not quite figured out how to use radar. The Japanese committed a large percentage of their naval land-based radar tracking units to New Britain and New Ireland, but the radar was only used to alert airfields to incoming enemy aircraft. Little attempt was made to use radar to vector aircraft to targets.

Japanese radar may have ended up serving the Allies more than the Japanese. During December 1943 and January 1944 Allied fighter sweeps invariably approached at altitudes high enough for radar to detect. This ensured that Japanese fighters – the object of a fighter sweep – would be in the air to meet the intruders. When surprise was desired bombers approached low,

The day after the battle of Empress Augusta Bay the Fifth Air Force attacked Simpson Harbor. Successful against transports and light warships, they were less successful against larger warships. The heavy cruiser *Haguro* is shown under attack; it escaped serious damage. (USNHHC)

Rabaul's Army garrison was largely untouched. Four times the expected number of Japanese troops surrendered at war's end. Among the material surrendered were nearly 100 Japanese light and medium tanks here photographed in a park near Rabaul. (AC)

This Kittyhawk (the export version of the P-40) was at one time flown by Geoff Fisken, New Zealand's highest-scoring fighter pilot. (Courtesy of the Tri-State Warbird Museum)

sometimes at wave-top level, to avoid radar detection. Alternatively, when approaching from high altitudes they would change course abruptly and attack from an unexpected direction avoiding the fighters heading to their original position. Since Japanese fighters lacked radios, they received no updates. Both tactics achieved surprise at critical battles.

History always seems inevitable in retrospect. The Japanese were close to winning the aerial siege of Rabaul on at least one occasion, however. The Allied victory was predicated on building airfields on Bougainville. There was no other place within single-engine fighter coverage of the advanced Allied airfields in the Solomons (such as Munda) and also within single-engine aircraft range of Rabaul.

The campaign's turning point came when Halsey committed his only two aircraft carriers to attack Rabaul on November 5. That attack damaged five of six Japanese heavy cruisers in Simpson Harbor. There were only four light cruisers available to protect the Allied invasion fleet. Had the Japanese cruisers sortied on the evening of November 5 the invasion fleet would probably have been destroyed, and the Marines could have been pushed off their beachhead. The loss would have prevented construction of Torokina and Piva airfields and occupation of the Green Islands, and would possibly have discouraged the landings at Arawe and Cape Gloucester.

While the Fifth Air Force's October air campaign had been spectacular, it had been indecisive. Nor is it likely that continued attacks with just B-24s, B-25s, and P-38s would have yielded the results achieved by the introduction of single-engine fighters and light bombers.

Sieges are won through attrition. So was Rabaul. Once the Allies were established on Bougainville and could bring enough force against Rabaul's air garrison, Japanese resistance eventually collapsed. Ultimately Japan's failure was due to its flawed doctrine. Japanese doctrine called for victory won through one decisive blow. This principle acknowledged Japanese industrial weakness. If Japan failed to win quickly it would eventually be crushed by the industrial capacity of its primary foe, the United States. It was the philosophy underpinning the attack on Pearl Harbor. It was the concept behind minimal protection for Japanese aircraft. Get in a blow first, hard enough, and your foe cannot strike back.

Yet it was virtually impossible to land a true knockout blow in one battle. Even decisive victories, such as Pearl Harbor, left most of the enemy's capabilities undamaged. No pilot could guarantee a kill on a first pass, leaving an opportunity for a counterattack. The one opportunity for a "one decisive blow" Japanese victory during the Rabaul campaign was stop-punched by the US Navy's November 5 air raid. Ironically the attack sank no warships. All but one was still capable of steaming, but none were battle-worthy.

Japan ended up locked into an attrition battle it was unprepared to win, yet could not avoid. It compounded its problem by taking no steps to mitigate its losses, priming its pilots to die trying rather than surviving to fight another day, and failing to train its pilots to fight as a team, rather than see themselves as individual samurai. Meanwhile the Allies had dedicated aircraft to rescue downed pilots, provided replacement aircraft, and emphasized teamwork.

Rabaul was the first Allied campaign where airpower substituted for ground occupation. The campaign was so successful it formed the pattern for future Allied campaigns. Except where geography required (such as the Marianas and Iwo Jima) or sentiment dictated (the Philippines) Japanese strongholds were isolated by air and bypassed. Hundreds of thousands of Japanese fighting men sat out the late stages of the war as spectators.

Bypassing Japanese strongholds shortened the war by years. Instead of "Golden Gate by '48," GIs were able to come "Home alive by '45." Airpower reached its apogee with the strategic bombing campaign against Japan in 1945. As at Rabaul, once US bombers could reach the Japanese Home Islands they were able to immobilize and isolate Japan to the point where – with the encouragement of atomic bombs delivered by air – it surrendered without requiring Allied ground forces on Japanese soil to force surrender.

Surviving aircraft

It is possible to find examples of the aircraft types which fought in the Rabaul campaign in museums throughout the world. This is especially true of the US aircraft built in thousands or tens of thousands: B-25s, P-38s P-40s, F6Fs, F4Us, and TBFs. There are plenty of aircraft such as the SBD or SB2C and the B-24. Sometime survivors number in the scores, even 70-plus years after World War II ended.

Japanese aircraft are more difficult to find. Thirty-plus Mitsubishi A6M variants are on display throughout the world. One Aichi D3A is undergoing restoration in California and two unrestored D3As are at the Nimitz Museum in Fredericksburg, Texas. There are no complete G4Ms or B5Ns on display although there are two partial examples of each. In some cases the "survivor" Zeroes suffer from George Washington's Axe syndrome. (We've replaced the head twice and the handle five times, but otherwise it is the exact same axe used by George Washington.) They are made up of bits and pieces of multiple Zeroes or consist mainly of replica parts added to replace missing pieces.

What is harder is finding existing aircraft which actually fought in the skies in or around Rabaul. Most of these seem to be in museums in Australia, New Zealand, and Papua New Guinea, especially examples of Allied aircraft. The B-25D displayed at Australian Aviation Heritage Centre flew with the 345th Bomb Group, which participated in the campaign. A B-25C and B-25D on display in Papua New Guinea are probably also Rabaul veterans. The SBD on display at the National Museum of WWII in New Orleans was a veteran of the Guadalcanal campaign, but missed Rabaul. It was sent to Chicago as a training aircraft, but crash-landed in Lake Michigan. It was later recovered and restored.

Perhaps the best example of a surviving warbird from the campaign is an RNZAF Kittyhawk, now in the possession of the Tri-State Warbird Museum in Batavia, Ohio. Flown by Geoff Fisken, the RNZAF's highest-scoring ace in World War II, this aircraft fought in the Solomons, almost certainly participating in RNZAF actions during the Rabaul campaign. It is being restored to flying condition. The Tri-State Warbird Museum also has a Corsair, an Avenger, and a B-25 on display, although these aircraft did not participate in the campaign.

Surprisingly, examples of Japanese aircraft that participated in the fight for Rabaul exist. Since the 1960s a small industry has emerged in recovering wrecked Japanese aircraft in New Guinea, the Solomon Islands, and New Britain. The Australian War Memorial Museum in Canberra, Australia has an A6M2 on display restored from a wreck. It was flown by Saburo Sakai at Lae. The Australian War Memorial Museum recovered several Zeroes at Rabaul in the 1970s. One was on display as a wrecked aircraft at Fantasy of Flight in Polk City, Florida.

FURTHER READING
AND BIBLIOGRAPHY

The best popular account of the siege of Rabaul comes from the final two books of Bruce Gamble's Rabaul trilogy, *Fortress Rabaul* and *Target Rabaul*. The first of the trilogy, *Invasion Rabaul*, describes the Japanese invasion of the Bismarck Archipelago. The other two, especially *Target Rabaul*, describe the struggle for the island and the Allied neutralization of the bastion. All three are worth reading both as history and as literary masterpieces.

My preference is using primary sources and official histories. Thanks to the Internet many sources which would have been difficult to locate 25 years ago are available digitally. Some make for dry reading or are highly technical, but I found them invaluable. Two periodicals which proved especially valuable were *US Army–Navy Journal of Recognition* and *Intelligence Bulletin*. Both were periodicals printed by the War Department in World War II, and circulated among those in uniform. They can be found on www.archive.org, as can all books with an asterisk following them.

I also used several memoirs. They can be useful, but must be used with your baloney detector turned up to 11. Participants on both sides tend not to let the truth get in the way of a good story.

The principal sources used for this book are:

Craven, Wesley Frank and Cate, James Lea (editors), *The Army Air Forces In World War II, Volume Four: The Pacific: Guadalcanal to Saipan, August 1942 to July 1944*, Office of Air Force History, Washington, DC, 1983*

Gamble, Bruce, *Target: Rabaul: The Allied Siege of Japan's Most Infamous Stronghold, March 1943–August 1945*, Zenith Press, Minneapolis, Minnesota, 2013

Gamble, Bruce, *Fortress Rabaul: The Battle for the Southwest Pacific, January 1942–April 1943*, Zenith Press, Minneapolis, Minnesota, 2010

Hirrel, Leo, *Bismarck Archipelago*, US Army Center of Military History, Washington, DC, 1994*

Japan committed sophisticated military electronics and communications systems to Rabaul. This radio direction-finding station at Rabaul provided directional information about Allied ships, aircraft, and shore installations. (USNHHC)

Hough, Frank O. and Crown, John A., *The Campaign On New Britain*, Historical Branch Headquarters US Marine Corps, Washington, DC, 1952*

Kawato, Masajiro (Mike), *Flight Into Conquest*, KNI Incorporated, Anaheim, CA, 1978

Kenney, George C., *General Kenney Reports: A Personal History of the Pacific War*, Duell, Sloan, and Pearce, New York, NY, 1949*

Miller, John, *Cartwheel: The Reduction of Rabaul*, Washington, Office of the Chief of Military History, Dept. of the Army, Washington, DC, 1959*

Morison, Samuel Eliot, *Breaking the Bismarcks Barrier: 22 July 1942–1 May, 1944* (*History of United States Naval Operations in World War II*, Vol. 6), Little, Brown, and Company, New York, NY, 1950

Nakagawa, Yasuzo, *Japanese Radar and Related Weapons*, Aegean Park Press, Laguna Hills, California, 1997

Sakaida, Henry, *The Siege of Rabaul*, Phalanx Publishing Co, Ltd., St Paul, Minnesota, 1996

Shaw, Henry I., Jr and Kane, Douglas T., *Isolation of Rabaul: History of U.S. Marine Corps Operations in World War II*, Volume II, Historical Branch, G–3 Division, Headquarters, US Marine Corps, Washington, DC, 1963*

United States Strategic Bombing Survey, *The Allied Campaign Against Rabaul*, Washington, DC, 1946

United States Strategic Bombing Survey, *The Fifth Air Force in the War Against Japan*, Washington, DC, 1947*

INDEX